The
Marquis
de Custine
and His
RUSSIA IN
1839

The
Marquis de
Custine
and His
RUSSIA IN 1839

BY

GEORGE F. KENNAN

PRINCETON UNIVERSITY PRESS

PRINCETON, NEW JERSEY

1971

Copyright © 1971 by
PRINCETON UNIVERSITY PRESS
ALL RIGHTS RESERVED
LCC 75-143818
ISBN 0-691-05187-9

This book has been composed in Linotype Caledonia
Printed in the United States of America
by Princeton University Press
Princeton, N.J.

Publication of this book has been
aided by the Whitney Darrow
Publication Reserve Fund of
Princeton University
Press.

CONTENTS

ILLUSTRATIONS

Custine in 1846, aquarelle by the Comtesse de Menou. (Reproduced by permission of the publisher from *Astolphe de Custine* by the Marquis de Luppé, Éditions du Rocher, Monaco, 1957)

Title page of the first edition of *La Russie en 1839*. (Reproduced by permission of the General Research Collections of the New York Public Library, Astor, Lenox, and Tilden Foundations)

FOLLOWING PAGE 34

Prince Pyotr Borisovich Kozlovski, caricature, ? 1813. (Reproduced from Gleb Struve, *Russki Evropeyets*, San Francisco, 1950)

Alexander Turgenev. (Bettmann Archive)

FOLLOWING PAGE 50

PREFACE

IN JANUARY of the year 1843 there was published in Paris, in four volumes, a book entitled *La Russie en 1839*. The author was a French nobleman of distinguished lineage, Astolphe Louis Léonor, Marquis de Custine. The book was an account of the impressions gained, and the reflections inspired, by a visit the Marquis had paid to Russia in the summer of 1839. It was at once a sensational success. Within a few years it ran through at least six legitimate French editions. It was promptly pirated and republished, in several editions, in Brussels. German and English translations, or condensations, followed shortly.* Although it was not published at that time in the Russian language, and was indeed immediately banned in Russia, French editions leaked into that country almost at once. They were read by Russians everywhere with avid interest, and with feelings that covered the spectrum of reaction from reluctant appreciation to violent indignation. Alexander Herzen, laying the work down after the first reading, pronounced it the best book ever written about Russia by a foreigner; but he then characteristically fell into despair at the thought that it had taken a foreigner to write it—that no Russian could have done it. The Emperor Nicholas I is said to have flung the volume to the floor in anger after perusing the first few pages, moaning something to the effect that "I am alone to blame; I encouraged and patronized the visit of this scoundrel." Later, though, it seems that curiosity got the better of him and that he read considerable parts of it aloud to his family in the long dull evenings of palace life.

Not only did the book thus strongly affect people then alive, but it demonstrated a most stubborn longevity. Some forty years later, despite the initial ban on publication in Russia, excerpts of it began to appear in Russian historical-archival series.* Nearly seventy years later, in 1910, an abridged translation of the entire work was published in Russia.¹ Another edition followed after the Russian Revolution, although that, too, was soon suppressed—for reasons which will surely become apparent in the course of this account.² In the 1930's and 40's, excerpts from the book were rediscovered and read with exquisite delight by western diplomats serving in Moscow, including myself. And when, in 1951, 108 years after its original appearance, a new abridged English translation appeared on the market, it contained a foreword written by a recent American Ambassador to the Soviet Union, and the translation itself had been done by the wife of a future such ambassador. (In neither case was the ambassador himself.)†

This casual diplomatic acquaintance sufficed to arouse my interest in Custine's work; and when, in 1963, I was asked to lecture at the University of Belgrade (in Serbian, for my sins) I chose, for want of a better subject, a comparison of Custine's visit to Russia with the similar journey of Tocqueville to the United States earlier in that same decade, and of the two books to which, respectively, those journeys led. This experience not only increased my interest in Custine but heightened my awareness of some of the

¹ For numbered references, see the note section at the end of the book, pp. 135ff.

* See *Russkaya Starina*, vol. LXI (1891), article by N. K. Schilder, for which reference I am indebted to the kindness of Professor Gleb Struve.

† The volume referred to here is *Journey for our Time* (New York, Pellegrini and Cudahy, 1951), a condensation of Custine's work edited and translated by Phyllis Penn Kohler. It was based on the third Amyot edition. The foreword was written by General Walter Bedell Smith, who had been American Ambassador in Russia from 1946 to 1949. Mrs. Kohler is the wife of Mr. Foy Kohler, who held this same ambassadorial office some years later, from 1962 to 1966.

mysteries and *lacunae* still then present in the historical record relative to his person and his journey.

In 1969, while spending some months as a visiting fellow at All Souls College in Oxford, I was asked to deliver there the Chichele Lectures, a series given annually under the auspices of that college. Faced with the problem of finding a suitable subject for an audience formidable in its erudition and general distinction and yet not united by any single field of scholarly interest, I considered first an elaboration of this same comparison between Custine and Tocqueville. I soon realized, however, that for me to regale an Oxford audience with reflections on Tocqueville and his *Democracy in America* would be to carry a load of singularly unimpressive and unwanted coals to Newcastle. I therefore decided to concentrate on Custine and his book, but to go into the subject in greater depth and detail than I had done before. This necessitated both a careful reading (the first I had given it) of the work itself and a serious effort of inquiry into the life of the author and the background of this particular literary effort. The lectures themselves offered only a very limited possibility for presentation of the results of this study, and it occurred to me, this being the case, that in view of the dearth of English-language material on the subject, a monograph bringing together the results of this small labor of research might fill a humble but respectable place in the historical record and be of value to such other scholars as may, from time to time, wish to know what *is* known about Custine and his book.

It is this modest purpose which the present volume is designed to serve, and the reader should not approach it with the expectation that it will serve any more exalted one. Since, however, Custine's book is still the subject of considerable feeling and controversy—since several of my Russian acquaintances hold in fact so low an opinion of Custine that they have tended to reproach me for giving him even this much attention—I have thought it right to append, as the final chapter, a brief discussion of the book's significance as I see it, a discussion which may serve as my apology for the effort involved.

If there be taken into consideration the existing secondary works in the French language, rather than just those that exist in English, I can claim no great originality for this account. In addition to the support derived from two small but valuable works of a biographical nature about Custine, both published in Monaco (rather obscurely, I fear; one was not available at all in the Oxford libraries) in the late 1950's,* [3] I found myself greatly and unexpectedly aided by the recently published doctoral dissertation of a scholar (now a professor) at the Sorbonne, M. Michel Cadot, entitled *La Russie dans la vie intellectuelle française, 1839-1856* (Paris, Fayard, 1967). This excellent work, the product of a formidable volume of painstaking research, takes off, chronologically, from Custine's journey and includes two long chapters (they constitute a book in themselves and are so described in the table of contents) on that journey and its literary product—chapters which represent without question the most exhaustive study ever made of this subject. In the third and fourth chapters of the present work, in particular, I have followed faithfully in paths already marked out by M. Cadot (I had, indeed, little choice, for there were so few paths he had left unexplored); and I must record at once the great extent of my indebtedness to him for his thorough work of pioneering. Without this support my own account would have been, I am sure, much poorer, and it would have taken longer to produce it. My excuses for retreading so much of the ground he has been over are only that his work is not yet widely known, or even easily available, beyond the reaches of a limited and highly-specialized sector of the French academic com-

---

* These were: *Marquis de Custine, Souvenirs et portraits. Textes choisis et présentés par Pierre de Lacretelle*, Monaco, Éditions du Rocher, 1956; and Marquis de Luppé, *Astolphe de Custine*, Monaco, Éditions du Rocher, 1957. See reference note 3 for additional information.

munity, that it is not available in English translation, and finally that the high degree of condensation of material and presentation by which it is marked render it more useful to professional students of the history of French literature than to a more general public interested primarily in the relation of Custine's book to the Russia of this present age.

I must further acknowledge my indebtedness to a number of people who have given assistance either with my research or with the presentation of it, or both: to M. Jules-Marie Priou, Director of the Bibliothèque de l'Assemblée Nationale in Paris, and his assistant, Madame Pierre Moinot, for their kind hospitality and assistance; to Madame Maria Daniliewicz and her collaborators in the Polish Library in London for their similar support; to Madame Grethe Larsen, of the Royal Library at Copenhagen, for helpful information on the Danish edition of Custine's work; to Mr. John P. Baker and the General Research Collection of the New York Public Library, Astor, Lenox, and Tilden Foundations, for permission to reproduce the title page of the first edition of *La Russie en 1839* (Paris, Amyot, 1843); to the Rockefeller Foundation, for its extension of the hospitality of the Villa Serbelloni as a refuge for the writing of the original lectures; to Professor L. R. Lewitter, of the University of Cambridge, for valuable bibliographical help with relation to Mickiewicz and Chaadayev; to my friend, Professor Robert C. Tucker, of Princeton University, for the loan of his copy of the very rare Soviet (1930) condensation of *La Russie en 1839*; to Mr. Igor Vinogradoff, for his interest in my researches and his permission to quote from his interesting memorandum; to Professors Gleb Struve of the University of California at Berkeley, and Ira Wade at Princeton, for their kindness in reading the manuscript and giving me helpful comment on many individual points; to my two research assistants, Mrs. Richard Ullman and Miss Janet Smith, for much patient searching of libraries and running-down of facts; to All Souls College for hospitality while the Chichele Lectures were being prepared, and above all to its Warden, John Sparrow, for his warm interest and support and for his personal kindness in procuring and presenting to me a copy of the rare third edition of Custine's work—a possession which I should have prized in any case for the sentiments that prompted its gift, but which was also of great help to me in the writing of this book.

I might just add that I do not consider this treatise to be in any way definitive. There are a number of mysteries that remain to be solved in connection with Custine's experiences in Russia, and my own judgments, I know, are far from exhausting the number of interpretive appreciations which this subject invites. It is my hope that the following discussion, incomplete as it is, will stimulate further exploration of the subject by scholars whose greater youth, more exuberant energies, and lesser burden of distracting interests and responsibilities will take them further along this path of discovery than I have been able to go.

G.F.K.

Princeton, N.J.
Autumn 1970

The
Marquis
de Custine
and His
*RUSSIA IN
1839*

I. *THE MAN*

ASTOLPHE DE CUSTINE was a man of good family, even by the more fastidious standards of his own day. On his father's side, the family was a wealthy Lotharingian one, in which the marquisal title had been passed down (rather casually, to be sure) since the early eighteenth century. Astolphe's grandfather had purchased the well-known porcelain factory at Niderwiller in the Haute-Lorraine (now part of the Department of the Moselle); and it was in the chateau at that place that the boy grew up. His mother was a Sabran— the child, that is, of one of the great noble families of France.[1]

Custine's own childhood was agitated and tragic in the extreme. He was born in 1790, on the eve of the most harrowing period of the French Revolution. He might be described, as we shall see presently, as himself an emotional casualty of the Terror. His relatively young paternal grandfather, a man then only in his late forties, had sympathized with the Revolution in its early stages and had become a general in the revolutionary armies. His name will be remembered as that of the commander of the armies on the Rhine. This service to the Revolution did not, however, save him from the Terror. In 1792, he was recalled, imprisoned, and finally guillotined. His young son, Astolphe's father, then only in his twenties, rose gallantly to his own father's defense, and was guillotined in his turn. Astolphe's mother, who had stood loyally by her young husband, visiting him in prison down to the last night, was herself taken and thrown into the death house after his execution. She escaped only narrowly, almost miraculously, the fate of her father-in-law and her husband.

All this happened when the boy, Astolphe, was only two or three years old. The house, meanwhile, was raided and sealed by the revolutionary police. The family fortune was confiscated. A faithful maidservant, a young peasant girl from Lorraine, took the child and cared for it in the one unsealed room of the house, which was the kitchen.

The mother was eventually released, came home, and set about with great resolution and ultimate success to restore the family fortunes. She was without question a remarkable person—a woman of great beauty, charm, and strength of character. Widely known under her first name of Delphine, she enjoyed a reputation and a general respect in French society greater than anything ever accorded in their time to her son. Madame de Staël took her name, precisely with a view to immortalizing it, as the title of one of her own novels. Delphine was for many years the intimate friend—the mistress, one must suppose—of the writer and statesman, Chateaubriand. The little boy was in fact brought up in part under the shadow of this impressive figure, whom he claims to have regarded as a sort of foster-father. But Chateaubriand's was not, unfortunately, the only male figure, and not even the only distinguished one, that fluttered around the candle of Delphine's great beauty, and it could not replace, emotionally, that of the missing father.

The boy thus remained throughout his youth the object of all the affection, attention, and protective patronage that a beautiful, high-powered, and solitary mother was capable of lavishing upon a beloved only son.* One cannot blame her; he was in a sense all she had. But it is clear that this unbalanced relationship, coming on top of the trauma of violent separation from both parents in early childhood, was too much for the boy's normal emotional development. He grew up handsome, brilliant, sensitive, delicate in

---

* Custine had had an older brother, Gaston, born in 1788. After being inoculated against smallpox, Gaston died in July 1792.

health, in many ways talented, but with a latent, at first subconscious and repressed but ultimately overpowering, homosexual orientation.

For long—out of respect, I suppose, for his mother—Custine contrived to lead an outwardly normal life. At the time of the Restoration, his mother wangled for him a military commission in one of the guard regiments. For a few weeks he trailed miserably around after his unit, buttoned into an uncomfortable uniform, a great sword clanking incongruously at his side; but he obviously failed to enjoy it, and was soon relieved of this duty. An effort was also made to use him as an aide to Talleyrand at the Congress of Vienna. But it was not long in becoming apparent that he was little better fitted for diplomacy than for life at court. His primary interest was literary. He became an enthused romantic, after the fashion of the day. The great figures of German literary romanticism formed the focus of his admiration. Some of them—including Heine, Varnhagen von Ense, and Varnhagen's remarkable wife, Rahel—became his warm personal friends.

In the early 1820's Custine acquiesced, amiably enough, in a marriage arranged for him by his mother. He became very fond, actually, of his young wife—even had a child by her. But when, in 1823, she—to his genuine and deep sorrow—suddenly died, something gave way within him. The effort to lead a conventional life failed. Other impulses, too long repressed, broke through with great and dangerous violence.

On the night of October 28, 1824, catastrophe ensued. Custine's unconscious and misused person was found that night, lying in the mud on the road from Versailles to St. Denis, stripped to the waist, beaten, robbed, the fingers broken, the ring ripped off. The deed had been done by a group of common soldiers with one of whom, allegedly, Custine had attempted to have a rendezvous.

Whether this was or was not the truth makes little difference. All of Paris believed that it was. The scandal was immense and spectacular. The whole affair came at once into the newspapers. Custine's reputation and his position in society were damaged beyond repair. From this time on to the end of his life he would figure, in the cruel gossip of the day, primarily as France's most distinguished and notorious homosexual.

The plight to which this personal catastrophe consigned him has been perhaps best described by Pierre de Lacretelle, in the introduction to the small volume of Custiniana which he published in 1956: "Imperturbable, le Marquis de Custine glissera désormais parmi les chuchotements, les sourires furtives, les regards moqueurs, méprisé par les uns, pris en pitié par les autres, problème pour tous."* The social rejection was cruel and drastic. One might note, as an example, the reaction of the Marquise de Montcalm, who responded to the news of the incident by sending word to Custine suggesting that he expiate his disgrace by a glorious death.

The episode of October 28, 1824 was only one of a series of disasters that overwhelmed Custine in just those years. He himself, in a letter to the Marquise de Montcalm, written (January 8, 1824) some months before his disgrace, described only the initial stage of this tragic series of events.[2] On January 7, 1823, according to this account, only a few months, that is, after the birth of Custine's small son, an old abbé, who had been a tutor to Custine's uncle and a virtual member of the family, died after pronouncing (Custine says he had lost his mind) a curse upon the entire family. Exactly six months later the young wife died, in terrible agony. At the lapse of just a year the same occurred with another member of the household—an old family friend. The child's nurse, meanwhile, had become insane. Successively, there perished everyone, except Custine himself and his mother, who had been connected with the wedding.

But Custine, writing that letter, did not yet know the

* *Marquis de Custine, Souvenirs et portraits. Textes choisis et présentés par Pierre de Lacretelle.* Monaco: Éditions du Rocher, 1956. The passage is difficult to translate. It might be rendered: "Henceforth the Marquis de Custine would make his way through life im-

full measure of the tragedy. Before that year of 1824 was out, there would come his own disgrace. Then, in the first days of 1826, his little son would die, and six months later his shattered and broken-hearted mother as well.*

Thrown back now upon himself, literally engulfed in humiliation, bereavement, and loneliness, Custine appears to have performed at this point an act of inner renunciation, and to have accommodated himself with relative dignity and reasonable success to his unhappy condition. He became calm and resigned where he had once been nervous and agitated. He learned to accept his exclusion from the aristocratic society of Paris. He sought fulfillment, for the rest of his life, in travel, in literature, and in religion. He had always been devout. His piety now received an even deeper foundation. He found in the serene paternalism of the Roman Church, in which he had been reared, not only the absolution and tolerance for his emotional abnormality which society had denied him, but a substitute for the guillotined father, and a replacement for the element of majesty and hierarchy which he so deeply missed in the public life of the France of his day.

This solace notwithstanding, Custine's life remained tragic and uncompleted. His emotional frailty hung everlastingly, like a stone, around his neck, weighing down his hopes, interfering with his personal relations, limiting at crucial points his creative literary power. This quality of his fate was well described by Madame Ancelot, in her *Les Salons de Paris*.† "Over everything that M. de Custine did," she wrote (pp. 239-240),

---

perturbably, amid whisperings, furtive smiles, and mocking glances, held in contempt by some, pitied by others, a problem for everyone."

* Delphine's epitaph was written, in effect, by the Marquise de Montcalm: "Je ne croyais pas . . . qu'on peut mourir de chagrin, et la pauvre Madame de Custine est la preuve du contraire."[3]

† Mme. Marguerite-Louise Virginie Chardon Ancelot (1792-1875) was the wife of the French man of letters and member of the Académie Française, Jacques-Arsène-François-Polycarpe Ancelot. They collaborated in the writing of *Reine, Cardinal et Page*, and other works. Mme. Ancelot wrote works for the theatre, novels (including *Emerance, Renée de Varville*), as well as *Les Salons de Paris*.

there hovered some baneful influence which diminished all his good fortunes. He united in himself, it is true, the greatest advantages of nature and society: he was tall and handsome, very spiritual, well-bred, extremely well educated, quite rich, and every inch the *grand seigneur* by ancestry, manners and feelings; but all these blessings did not prevent him from having a restless and tormented soul, which left him no peace. He was unable to find repose: he seemed driven by some inexplicable derangement of equilibrium which tore him away from everything that gave happiness to other men.

It must be noted that in the adjustment to his personal misfortunes and in the creation of a new life for himself Custine was decisively aided by the devoted attention and companionship of an English friend, Edward St. Barbe—Édouard de Sainte-Barbe, as he called himself in France. Sainte-Barbe, the son of a prominent family of Hampshire gentry with estates near Lymington on the south coast of England (the family traced its origins, and its French name, to a companion-in-arms of William the Conqueror), joined Custine, as a constant associate, shortly *before* (one notes this timing with a new tinge of pity for the parties to Custine's marital tragedy), the death of the young marquise. He then remained with Custine as a devoted companion and helper (Custine, in his private correspondence, often referred to him facetiously and affectionately as *"l'esclave"*) until Custine's death in 1857, running the household and bearing a large part of the burden of management of Custine's personal affairs. The *ménage à deux* which these two gentlemen conducted for over thirty years, transformed occasionally into a *ménage à trois* when —as happened more than once—Custine expended his hospitality and patronage for a time on some other male figure as well, was naturally the cause of much malicious merriment in Paris society. But contemporary witnesses who knew Sainte-Barbe are unanimous in the judgment that he was a man of great delicacy and distinction of character: loyal, self-effacing, and dignified, and that he carried his own part in this unusual arrangement with exemplary tact and discretion. He dedicated his life to Custine; and the latter's appreciation for this devotion is evident from an anguished reference to him, in a letter written by Custine to another friend when Sainte-Barbe was seriously ill in 1856, as *"un homme sans lequel je ne puis vivre."* It is clear that what was involved here was a profound, abiding, and in many ways touching relationship, going far deeper than could be explained by just those physical impulses to which a cynical Paris loved to ascribe it, and one which probably alone enabled Custine to endure his disgrace and to go forward with his life and his work as a literary person.

For the remainder of his life, Custine was seen primarily in literary circles. The literary salons of Paris, in contrast to the purely social ones, remained open to him—partly, no doubt, because his own hospitality was extended in the grandest and most lavish manner to prominent people of the literary world.* He was well acquainted with many of the great literary figures of the day: with Victor Hugo, George Sand, Balzac, Stendhal, Baudelaire, Lamartine, Sophie Gay. He was permitted to read aloud his own works in the salon of Madame Récamier, and Balzac paid him the compliment of doing the same *chez Custine.* Chopin played, on occasion, at his soirées.

None of these friendships, it seems, were close or lasting ones—except perhaps that with Sophie Gay. For this, Custine's lurid private life, and the different orientation of his deeper human attachments, constituted a barrier. It is also true that many who were outwardly on good terms

---

* Custine's great town house (6, Rue de la Rochefoucauld) once (before Custine) the residence of the sculptor Pigalle, has survived to this day, but only as part of the headquarters of the *Compagnie des Ateliers et Forges de la Loire.* The grand salon, with its ornate *Empire* ceiling and its lovely parquet-inlaid floors, where once Chopin played and Chateaubriand read aloud from his works, now serves as the company's board room; and in the similarly decorated dining-room, now cut up by partitions, typewriters clatter, and the doors bang as people carry papers in and out.

with him and accepted his hospitality were unable to resist the general tendency to sneer at him behind his back. But it is not too much to say that Custine was a well-known, if somewhat dubious, figure in the literary society of the Paris of his day.

To be recognized as a "real" writer—to be accepted as a major literary personality: this was Custine's greatest desire.* In the attempt to realize this ambition, he tried almost every form of literature. Poems, novels, drama: all these flowed at one time or another from his hopeful and aspiring pen. None was a disgraceful failure; none, on the other hand, was a serious success. In 1833, he contrived to have a play produced; but this was at great cost to himself (he literally bought the theatre for the purpose), and it was unceremoniously yanked from the repertoire after three performances. He was often accused, at least in the gossip of the day, of trying to bribe the critics and to buy favorable publicity; but if there was anything in these charges, the effort was singularly unsuccessful: the critics were seldom kind to him. Until the appearance of *La Russie en 1839* he had no great reputation. His friend Heine was able, with some justification, to damn him with the cutting description of *"un demi-homme de lettres."* It was *La Russie en 1839* that finally established him and gave him his reputation as a serious literary figure; and even here the success flowed from the reception of the book by the public, not from any particular appreciation for it on the part of the French critics, who, as we shall see, were divided and largely unenthusiastic.

In spirit and style, Custine was in the deepest sense a romantic. Everything he wrote was burdened with the characteristic affectations of this literary school. For him, as for all the other romanticists (but perhaps for better

---

* The Marquis de Luppé, in his biography, quotes Custine as saying, in a letter to Sophie Gay, after the success of *La Russie en 1839*: "I have had only one ambition in my life: to find a place among the good writers of my time and to be considered by them as one of themselves." *Astolphe de Custine*, p. 236.

reason than was commonly the case), it was the image of the noble, misunderstood individual, the unappreciated hero, that commanded the imagination and inspired the posture. He, like the others, ensconced himself figuratively on his own lonely pinnacle of pride and estrangement, hugging to his breast sensibilities which, you were permitted to feel, were too exquisite to stand full exposure to the gaze of an unfeeling world, prepared to let you glimpse or sense these sensibilities occasionally through the veils of reticence with which a noble nature required that they be obscured, but never prepared to inflict upon them the brutality either of disciplined analysis or of frank expostulation. This, if I am not mistaken, was, in part at least, what it meant to be a literary romanticist of the 1820's. Custine never wholly shook off this spirit. Its imprint rested on all that he wrote. It shines through at many points even in *La Russie en 1839.*

But the romantic spirit, as the history of literary taste has shown, was not in itself enough to make a great writer. It was often a handicap rather than an aid to creative immortality. It constituted a crust of intellectual and emotional convention which had to be broken through, as it was in the case of such men as Byron, Pushkin, Lermontov, and Walter Scott, by some deeper and stronger source of creative vitality, if greatness was to be achieved.

As a poet, a novelist, and a dramatist, Custine simply lacked this extra power. There was, however, one field where he was eventually able to develop it, and this was the travel account.

Custine adored travel. He spent a good part of his life in the pursuit of it. He found it, he says, *une douce manière de passer la vie* for one who was out of accord with the ideas of his time (he might have added: "and was rejected by the society into which he had been born"). He "read" countries, he claimed, as other people read books. Travel was, as he saw it, a means of changing not only scenes but centuries as well. What one had from it was *"l'histoire analysée dans ces résultats."* [4] It was in the travel account that his qualities, such as they were, came into their own.

I am not familiar with the first of his efforts along this line. They were sketches of travel in Switzerland, Italy, England, and Scotland—travel that had been performed when he was very young, but the account of which was not edited for publication until many years later.[5] I have heard this work criticized with extreme severity—as the most atrocious romantic nonsense, written much under the influence of the Ossian legend. A later work on Spain, published only a year before Custine embarked on his journey to Russia, was obviously a much more serious effort.[6] I have the impression that this last work was unjustly ignored by contemporaries and committed to oblivion by later generations; but of this, of course, only someone familiar with Spain and its history could be a proper judge.

With the account of the journey to Russia, in any case, such abilities as Custine possessed as a literary person came to their final fruition. Forty-nine years old when he performed the journey, and fifty-two when he began his account of it, he was now at the height of his powers. The stinging challenge of confrontation with Russian realities—a challenge that has evoked the best from more than one western observer over the course of the centuries—brought out all that he had it in him to give in the way of vigor of reaction. It drew on all his qualities, but above all on his moral discrimination, his sense of the fitness of things, and his feel-

---

* Quotations from the text of *La Russie en 1839*, such as this one, are taken from the second Amyot edition, of 1844, and are cited simply as *La Russie*, followed by the volume and page numbers. The translations are not of uniform origin. Some are my own. Some are taken *in toto* from the Longman English edition. Some are mixtures of the two: Where I have used language that was not my own I have tried to indicate this in the respective reference note. Where not otherwise indicated, the translation may be taken as my own, it being borne in mind that in some instances there was substantially only one normal way to translate the French phrase, and thus the two translations could coincide. I have not hesitated to translate liberally where this seemed necessary to convey something of the spirit and eloquence of the original.

ing for the essentials of a decent and hopeful civilization. In the confrontation with the Russia of Nicholas I, Custine's abilities as a writer, wasted for lack of real artistic talent when it came to other forms of literature, were finally permitted to find their ultimate realization.

La Russie en 1839 represented very nearly the culmination of Custine's literary career. He wrote one more novel, of mediocre success, did a bit more travelling—mostly to Italy, survived most of his friends, sold his Paris house, and finally, after sensing clearly the approach of death, died suddenly at his suburban home in St. Gratien, in September 1857, his passing almost unnoticed in a France which had long forgotten him. He was survived for only little more than a year by his faithful companion and heir, Sainte-Barbe. His papers appear to have been completely lost in a confused series of vicissitudes that included destruction of a part of them (no doubt on his own instructions) by Sainte-Barbe, bouts of litigation over the estates of both men, and much indifference, neglect, and even rumors of misuse for purposes of blackmail, on the part of later heirs and others. With the disappearance of these papers there were denied to the historian, we must suppose, the last important clues to the various mysteries surrounding the memorable journey which Custine had made to Russia nearly two decades before his death and for which, alone, his name continues to be known to later generations.

Astolphe de Custine cannot be classed a great man. The artificiality and narrowness of horizon that marked his upbringing; the inner timidity which he was often able to conceal but never really to overcome; the scars of his painful emotional experience; the romantic distortion in his view of reality: these posed tragic strictures on the degree to which he was able to develop what might, in other circumstances, have been talents approaching the level of greatness.

But Custine was, by anyone's standards, a man of unusual qualities. The overpowering influence of his mother, and the streak of effeminacy in his nature that resulted from it, had endowed him with intuitive powers beyond those common to members of his sex. With these were coupled a keen intellect, the best sort of classical education that the private tutoring of that age was able to give, the broadening effects of many years of travel, and a real passion for language and literature. Personal adversity, finally, had made of him a philosopher of sorts—had endowed him with a great sensitivity to moral values, a fine nose for cant and hypocrisy of every sort, and in certain respects an elevation of outlook that carried him well above some of the prejudices and conventions of his time. It was these qualities that he brought to the performance of his journey and to the drafting of his account of it.

II. *THE MOTIVES OF THE JOURNEY*

WHAT moved Custine to undertake the journey to Russia, and to undertake it at the time he did, is not wholly clear. But there are three points that deserve notice in this connection.

It was, first of all, only the previous year—1838—that had seen the publication of his four-volume work on Spain. He had been guilty of the most egregious delay in the writing and publication of that work. The journey on which the book was based had been performed in the year 1831. By the time the book appeared, the regime in Spain had changed and much of the subject matter had become out of date. It was this inordinate lapse of time between completion of the journey and publication of the account of it that obliged Custine to change the title of the work and to emphasize its historical quality by calling it *L'Espagne sous Ferdinand VII*. Despite this staleness in the subject matter, the book was relatively well-received by the critics —better than any of his previous works. This circumstance alone would have been sufficient to encourage him in the conclusion that the travel account—not the novel or the poem or the drama—was his true *forte*.

Beyond these connotations of the Spanish journey for Custine's concept of his true literary genre, there were also connotations relating to subject matter. No one was ever more profoundly a western-European than Custine. Everything about his tastes, his interests, his political philosophy, and his faith, had the deepest sort of roots in the history and culture of his native France, and, beyond that, in the traditions of the Roman Church and the Roman Empire. But Spain, as he himself at once recognized, was only partly a European country. His visit to it represented in a sense his first contact with the non-European world. He was keenly conscious of this fact, and highly sensitive to those subtle differences in thought and feeling and reaction that set Spain off from the Europe he knew. His success in spotting and describing these differences in *L'Espagne sous Ferdinand VII* inspired in him the thought of testing these same abilities by a visit to another semi-European country— Russia. He himself confessed this in so many words, in the text of his book on Spain. He was curious, he wrote, to compare Russia and Spain; both, he thought, constituting as they did only the extremities of the European continent, were more closely related to the Orient than any of the other nations of Europe.[1]

All of this would alone have been sufficient to permit us to ascribe the motivation for Custine's Russian journey in large measure to his experience with the book on Spain. But this effect, whatever it might otherwise have been, must have been immensely and spectacularly multiplied when he received, in August 1838, a letter from Balzac praising the book on Spain—a letter which would have turned the head of a man far less ambitious, and more successful, than Custine. One can imagine with what intense delight—greater, probably, than anything else experienced in his entire professional career as a writer—he must have read such phrases as these:

> . . . il y a peu de livres modernes qui puissent être comparés à ces lettres.

> Je ne dis cela qu'entre nous, car le livre sur l'Espagne est une oeuvre qui ne serait écrite par aucun des littérateurs de métier.

> Vous êtes le voyageur par excellence. Ce que vous faites me confond, car il me semble que je serais incapable d'écrire de semblables pages.

Words such as these, coming from the pen of the famous author of *Le Père Goriot* and *Le Lys dans la vallée*, must have come like nectar to the palate of Custine, who had no higher ambition in life than to receive just this sort of recognition; and they would alone have sufficed to assure the formation in his mind of an intention to perform further such journeys. But Balzac did not let it go at that. "Si vous faites," he added,

> la même chose sur chaque pays, vous aurez fait une collection unique en son genre, et qui aura le plus grand prix, croyez-moi. En ceci, je m'y connais. Je ferai tout ce qui sera en mon pouvoir pour vous engager à peindre ainsi l'Allemagne, l'Italie intérieure, *le Nord*, la Prusse. Ce sera un grand livre et une grande gloire.* [2]

* I have given these passages in the original French because only this can convey the effect they must have produced on Custine. A translation will be found in the reference notes for this chapter at the end of the book.

The acquaintance between Balzac and Custine had begun in the early thirties, when Balzac wrote appreciatively to Custine about one of the latter's early literary works—a favor which Custine returned, with interest, on the occasion of the one and only performance of Balzac's *Vautrin*. The two men met in Vienna, in 1835; and it was on that occasion that Custine made the acquaintance of Balzac's future wife, Madame Hanska. The pleasant relationship endured until the appearance of *La Russie en 1839*. Balzac, though often warned by others of Custine's lurid reputation, resolutely declined on grounds of principle to allow their relationship to be influenced by gossip about matters which he regarded as Custine's private affair. After Custine's visit to Russia, however, a concern on Balzac's part for Madame Hanska's financial and political interests in Russia caused him to distance himself from Custine—even to the point of forbidding Madame Hanska to write to Custine. When Balzac himself went to St. Petersburg, very shortly after the appearance of Custine's book, he toyed with the idea of writing something in the nature of a corrective to it. The coolness of his reception in Russia, however (on the Emperor's part, a result, no doubt, of the reaction to Custine's visit), together with the lessons of his own observations on the Russian scene, caused him to drop this idea entirely. When Balzac passed through Berlin, on his way back to western Europe after his sojourn in Russia, the French Ambassador in that city reported to the French government that the way Balzac talked about Russia sounded no different than the book by Custine. Madame Hanska, too, in whose experience with official Petersburg there was no lack of bitterness, appears to have had a high opinion of Custine's work.

I have taken the liberty of italicizing, in this passage, the words "le Nord," for this was, of course, the term used in France at that time to refer to Russia. We see from this that Custine had from Balzac not only the most warm encouragement to make the writing of travel accounts his true *métier* but also the specific suggestion that Russia be included among the countries to which he should address his talent. It seems inconceivable that, in setting about as he did less than half a year later to prepare a journey to Russia, Custine should not have been acting at least partially under the influence of these words.

The second of the factors that might be mentioned in connection with the motivation for Custine's journey to Russia is also one that cannot be proven. It has its existence, admittedly, only in the imagination of this writer. It is the example set for Custine, as an object of both admiration and emulation, by the appearance of the first volume of Tocqueville's *De la Démocratie en Amérique*.

This volume had appeared in 1835. Its immense success was one of the commanding phenomena of the French literary-political scene just in the years 1836 and 1837 when, presumably, Custine was drafting his work on Spain. That Custine read it, and that it made a deep impression on him, is evident not only from the fact that he enlivened the title page of *L'Espagne sous Ferdinand VII* with a quotation from it,* but also from the highly respectful mention of it, and discussion of some of Tocqueville's views, in Letter XXXI of that same book. He must have wished, as he completed his own book, that he could emulate it. But Spain, as a subject, was not a suitable counterpart of Tocqueville's America. Russia, on the other hand, was.

There is a strange sort of symmetry—in some respects that of precise similarity, in others of precise opposition—

---

* The quotation was: "Mon but n'a pas été de préconiser telle forme de gouvernement en général; car je suis du nombre de ceux qui croient qu'il n'y a presque jamais de bonté absolue dans les lois."

between the persons and the journeys of Custine and Tocqueville, within the same decade, to the two great developing outposts of European civilization: Russia and America. These two men were, first of all, the products of a very similar family tradition and experience. Both were aristocrats. Both families had suffered severely in the Terror of the recent Revolution. Both men, perhaps partly by way of reaction to these injustices and atrocities, had taken particularly to heart the values of the *ancien régime* to which their fathers had been attached. Both were disgusted by the decline of aristocratic institutions, and the corresponding advance of social equality, as forces in the life of France.

One of these men went West, to North America, determined to plunge to the core of these disturbing tendencies, to observe them in their most extreme, perhaps their most hideous, form—to see, in effect, the worst. The other went East, in search of a place where these tendencies were reputed not to be present at all, where older values might be expected to be found intact—to see, in other words, the best. Tocqueville, believing the strength of American democracy to lie in its local institutions, travelled almost exclusively in the provinces, greatly neglected the organs of central authority, visited Washington, in fact, only briefly, towards the end of his journey, and with only perfunctory interest. Custine, coming to a country where power was centralized as nowhere else in the Christian world, quite properly and naturally confined his attentions largely to the capital city, the court, and the central apparatus of government.

Yet from these disparate experiences the two men derived, as we shall see, almost identical political conclusions. Tocqueville drew them, so to speak, from the positive example, examining American democracy and finding it, while not the best of governments and not the one for which his own heart yearned, nevertheless a tolerable one—a species of dim half-world in which man, if lower than the angels, would still be higher than the beasts. Custine proved the same point by looking at the negative example: by seeing a bit, and sensing even more, of what modern despotism could become if it were to be modified neither by the power of an aristocracy nor by the representation of the people.

How much these men knew of each other's examples, I do not know. I doubt that Custine knew very much at all about the United States. What he did know, he presumably had primarily from Tocqueville. I sometimes wonder how he would have reacted had he gone there. As for Tocqueville, we are confronted with something of a mystery. He had no opportunity, of course, to read Custine's book before writing his own. There is almost no evidence generally in his work, or—I believe—in his correspondence, of any particular interest in Russia. Yet it will be recalled that he chose to end the first volume of his great book precisely with a passage of comparison of Russia and America, the prophetic power of which has caused it to be widely quoted ever since. The words of this passage that related to Russia could not have been better taken and phrased had they been written by a man long familiar with that country. One scarcely needs to recall them: the reference to the sudden rise to prominence of both Russia and America; the assertion that the two countries were only on the threshold of their real growth; and the remarkable analysis of the difference in the way the two peoples perceived their mission:

> The American struggles against the obstacles that nature opposes to him; the adversaries of the Russian are men. The former combats the wilderness and savage life; the latter, civilization with all its arms. The conquests of the American are therefore gained by the plowshare; those of the Russian by the sword. The Anglo-American relies on personal interest to accomplish his ends and gives free scope to the unguided strength and common sense of the people; the Russian centers all the authority of society in a single arm. The principal instrument of the former is freedom; of the latter, servitude. Their starting-point is different; yet

each of them seems marked out by the will of Heaven
to sway the destinies of half the globe.[3]

I have yet to find the explanation for the inclusion of this
remarkable passage in Tocqueville's work and for the emphasis he gave it by placing it at the end of the volume.
But that he was no less aware of the importance of Russia
in the coming scheme of things than of the importance of
the United States is obvious; and one suspects that for
Custine, consciously or unconsciously, these impressive
words may have served as the point of departure not only
for a voyage but for an intellectual adventure.

I have been at pains to discover whether Custine and
Tocqueville knew each other, and whether there was any
communication between them. It seems at first sight im-
plausible that they should not have done so. They had, it
would seem, a host of common acquaintances. Tocqueville,
just to take one example, was a cousin of Chateaubriand;
his childhood playmates, he tells us, were the Chateaubriand children. Custine, on the other hand, says that he,
in his childhood, regarded Chateaubriand, the devoted ad-
mirer of his mother, as a sort of foster-father. But we must
bear in mind that Tocqueville was by fifteen years the
younger of the two; and by the time he came to Paris and
began to circulate in the society of that city, Custine had
already suffered his personal catastrophe and disgrace, and
was no longer received in the best salons.

I can find nothing in Tocqueville's correspondence to
suggest the slightest interest in Custine, and I have evidence
of only one meeting between the two men. I suspect it was
the only one that ever took place. It occurred, probably in
the salon of Madame Récamier, after the completion of
Custine's journey to Russia but before he had gotten down
to the drafting of his account of it. It was mentioned in a
letter from Custine to Varnhagen von Ense, dated February
22, 1841. To Tocqueville, Custine must have appeared, in
the given circumstances, as a relatively obscure man, known
only for his inferior literary works and his reputedly scan-

dalous personal life. Tocqueville himself, on the other hand, was now at the height of his fame: the author of the celebrated *Démocratie en Amérique*, the second volume of which had just appeared, a member of the Chamber of Deputies, already a growing figure in French political life. He would, in this situation, have had very little interest in Custine; and indeed I have heard it said somewhere that he snubbed him most brutally on this occasion—whether intentionally or by lack of interest one is left to conjecture. Custine, on the other hand, fully aware of the great success of Tocqueville's work, having himself just performed a journey comparable to that of Tocqueville, and being now about to write his account of it, would have viewed the other man with the most intense interest. This is indeed reflected in the pen portrait of him that he sent to von Ense. "I have made the acquaintance," he wrote,

> of M. de Tocqueville, author of the *Démocratie Améri-caine*. He is a puny man, thin, short, and still young. He had about him a touch both of the old man and the child. He is the most naive of the ambitious ones. The way he looks at you is charming but it lacks frankness. He has a bilious color. His expressive face would captivate me more if it disturbed me less. One sees that he speaks with several meanings at once, and that his opinion is an instrument for the attainment of his ends.[4]

I doubt that Tocqueville ever read Custine's book, or took any interest in it, after it appeared. It was not in his nature. He had in high degree what we today would call the one-track mind. It was his custom to occupy himself only with one matter at a time; and when he did so, he preferred to pursue his own thoughts, learning what he could of the facts but not reaching out to inquire the opinions of others. He would probably not have paid any attention to Custine's book even had he decided, after its appearance, to make a study of Russia. Custine, observant man that he was, surely recognized this quality in Tocqueville; and one suspects it was this he had most prominently in mind when, shortly after their meeting, he included the following curious passage in the work he was then writing on Russia. It was a passage referring ostensibly to Montesquieu; but the characterization is in the plural, and the encounter with Tocqueville can scarcely have been absent from Custine's mind when he wrote it: " . . . ces grands esprits ne voient que ce qu'ils veulent; le monde est en eux; ils comprennent tout, hors ce qu'on leur dit."[5]

One can hear in these words, I suspect, the true reflection of the reaction—at once admiring, wistful, and resentful—with which Custine, a person long accustomed to snubs, must have pocketed this particular one from a man whom he obviously intensely admired.

Despite the symmetry of their respective experiences, these were, one senses, two very different people: Tocqueville—reserved, remote, spotlessly conventional and emotionally successful in private life, immensely respected everywhere, the darling, in fact, of the political and intellectual society of the Europe of his day—a man often alone but seldom, I think, lonely; Custine—a questionable character—a man with only a small and inferior reputation, hounded by failure and avoided by success—a man seldom alone, but always lonely. Tocqueville was intellectual and scientific in his tastes, little interested in the predicament or the behavior of man the individual, greatly interested—interested, in fact, with a serene, austere, monumental detachment—in the behavior of man in the mass. He was the true forerunner of the modern sociologist and political scientist at his best. Custine's interests, on the other hand, were aesthetic and religious. He was a very personal sort of man; and it was always the individual, not the multitude, on whom his eye was fixed.

The third factor affecting Custine's decision to go to Russia may have been, as some have professed to think, a major one, or it may have been, as I myself prefer to believe, of minor importance; but its existence, as a motive, is at least better documented than are the other two.

Among the Polish political exiles who took refuge in

France after the Polish uprising of 1830-31, there was one—
a very young man, dashing and handsome—whom Custine, beginning in 1835 and for a period of about five years
thereafter, took under his wing, befriended, supported fi-
nancially, and housed whenever he had no other place to
go. The young man in question was Ignace de Gurowski,
brother of the well-known Pan-Slavist Adam Gurowski
who, at a much later date, was to go to the United States,
to become a translator in the State Department, and to
annoy and alarm Lincoln with a series of violent letters
about policy questions during the Civil War.

That the attractiveness of Ignace's person had something
to do with the friendship and patronage Custine bestowed
upon him, one cannot doubt. Paris, of course, placed its
own interpretation on the relationship; and Ignace's residence in Custine's home was the principal occasion for
the many quips about the *ménage à trois*. Ignace, however,
had no lack of interest in the female sex; and such evidence
as exists of at least the latter years of this curious association between him and Custine suggests a paternal-filial
relationship—and one increasingly wearing and costly for
Custine as time went on—rather than the one read into it
by the gossips of the capital.

Ignace appears to have been an adventurer of sorts:
charming and amusing no doubt (Custine often mentions
these qualities in his correspondence with others) but
shallow, egotistical, cold, and vulgar. He cost Custine, before the relationship wore itself out, not only a great deal
of money but also considerable personal embarrassment.
Jilted by the actress Rachel, to whom he induced Custine
to make a proposal of marriage on his behalf (this was in
1842, after Custine's trip to Russia), he got himself into
trouble by attacking physically an elderly peer of France
whom he suspected of having inspired the lady's distaste
for himself, and then compromising, and finally eloping
with—and marrying—the Infanta Isabelle, niece of the
Queen of Spain. (This marriage, begun in poverty and in
exile in Belgium, endured for many years; and Ignace is

said to have ended his days as a Spanish grandee and the father of many children.)

In the period 1838-39, Gurowski was desirous of obtaining permission to return to the Russian Empire and to live there, as his brother Adam was then doing. Custine, it is clear, was anxious to help him in the realization of this aspiration (in the hopes, some think, of being rid of him at long last); and he made, in connection with his own journey, several efforts in this direction, including introducing Gurowski to the Russian Crown Prince while passing through Germany on the way to Russia; then taking the matter up personally in Russia with the Empress; and finally, after return from Russia, presenting Gurowski to the Empress on one of the latter's periodic visits to a German spa.

Actually, the acquaintance with Gurowski was not without its relation to Custine's experience in Russia; for Gurowski had a half-sister at the Russian court—the wife of the Master of the Horse, Baron Frederiks; and it was at least in part through her intercession that Custine was received by the Emperor and shown various other courtesies at court on the occasion of his visit there.*

As indicated above, there are some who have seen in Custine's desire to help Gurowski to return to Russia the main motivation for his journey, and have attributed to mortification over the failure of this effort (for the permission was never granted) the captious and critical tenor of his book. This strikes me, I must say, as quite improbable. As the Marquis de Luppé has pointed out, Gurowski already had a friend at the Russian court, and one extremely well-placed for such an intervention, in the per-

---

* Baroness Frederiks, née Cecilia Gurowska, was a daughter of Count Ladisław Gurowski by his first wife. She had been brought up together with the Russian Empress Charlotte Louise, at the court of the latter's father, the Prussian King Frederick William III, and was thought by some to be a natural child of the King. She served the Russian Empress for many years in Petersburg as a lady-in-waiting. According to the Marquis de Luppé, her position at the Russian court suffered severely, as did that of her husband, as a result of the appearance of Custine's book.

son of his half-sister; and Custine's visit was not really necessary as a means of bringing to the attention of the Imperial couple Gurowski's desire to return. But beyond this, such a thesis appears, with all due allowance for Custine's many faults and deficiencies, to do less than justice to his seriousness as a traveller, a writer, and a philosopher. *La Russie en 1839*, even after the recognition of its many blemishes, inaccuracies, and deficiencies, is too much of a book to be put down merely to Custine's interest in a young Polish friend, and particularly one of whose many limitations of character he could not, by this time, have been unaware.

Custine's connection with Gurowski, nevertheless, has a more than negligible importance for the understanding of his book, because it had its place in the extensive pattern of Polish influences by which Custine, both before and after his journey, was affected. Young Gurowski was, of course, only one—and a very obscure one—of the many, and in part distinguished, Polish figures who had fled their native country and taken up residence in Paris at the time of the uprising of 1830-31. These people were of course anti-Russian to a man; and they did not hesitate to recommend themselves to the French as experts on Russia and authorities on the iniquities of Russian power. Nor was their expertise on this subject to be underrated. As my friend Sir Isaiah Berlin once observed to me in this connection: "Victims make acute observers."

How many of these Paris Poles Custine knew is difficult to establish. He was seen at the salon of Princess Czartoryska, whose husband, Prince Adam Czartoryski, was the most distinguished and influential figure in this wave of Polish emigration. With Chopin, as we have seen, as well as with Chopin's friend, George Sand, he was well acquainted. It was a Pole, Eugène de Breza, who brought him together with Heine, and who, much later—in the mid-1840's—published a small volume of his own correspondence with another Pole, Countess Radolinska, in the title of which Custine's name figured prominently.* Custine's acquaintance with Madame Hanska—the Polish object of Balzac's affections—has already been mentioned.

But of all the Polish émigrés in Paris who exercised an influence on Custine we are safe, I believe, in assigning first place to the great poet Adam Mickiewicz. The late Professor Wacław Lednicki stated, in his *Russia, Poland and the West*,[6] that Custine had met Mickiewicz before his trip to Russia and had read his poems.† It is also quite possible that Custine, before entering on the writing of his book on Russia, had heard one or more of Mickiewicz' first series of lectures at the Collège de France.‡ There is, however, no proof of this; and indeed there is no evidence that

* The little volume in question, entitled *Monsieur le Marquis de Custine en 1844. Lettres adressées à Madame la Comtesse Josephine Radolinska par Eugène de Breza*, and published in 1845 by Librairie Étrangère, in "Leipsick," is surely one of the oddest of bibliographical curiosities. The words "par Eugène de Breza" are carried in such small type on the title page that a casual glance would give the impression that these were letters from Custine to the lady in question. The volume turns out, however, to contain, without any introduction and indeed without the slightest explanation of the reason for their publication, seven letters addressed by the unidentified Eugène de Breza to the equally unidentified countess in the period from September 1 to October 2, 1844. All are written from various places around the shores of Lake Geneva—two from St. Gingolph, which was often visited by Custine. Despite the book's title, only three of the letters make any reference to Custine. In one of these cases, the reference is wholly incidental. In the other two, an effort is obviously made, for reasons quite unclear, to commend Custine, by the most flowery and elaborate praises, to the favor of the lady, who evidently did not know him personally. The remaining letters are unexceptional personal ones, having nothing to do with Custine and no visible merits, literary or otherwise, that would justify their publication. The reader is left completely mystified as to the reasons for the whole procedure.

† Professor Lednicki did not cite a source for this statement. Custine and Mickiewicz had so many common acquaintances (one thinks particularly of the Russian-born but Catholic salon-hostess, Madame de Circourt) that it would have been surprising if they had not met at some point. At one point in his book (II, 229) Custine indicates a familiarity with Mickiewicz' work by comparing him with Pushkin.

‡ These lectures began on December 20, 1840. Custine was then very much in Paris. A number of his friends are known to have been in attendance.

the two men were ever personally close or that Custine was greatly affected by any conversations he may have had with Mickiewicz.

The manner in which Mickiewicz is most likely to have influenced *La Russie en 1839* is through his writings. The first volume of a French translation of Mickiewicz' works, prepared by Christian Ostrowski, was published in Paris in 1841, just as Custine was getting down to the writing of his book.* [7] This volume included the *Digression*, written in Dresden in 1832, one of the six parts of which was the bitterly anti-Russian *Road to Russia*. Such was Mickiewicz' fame in Paris at that time, and so numerous and close were the bonds of common acquaintance linking the two men, that Custine could scarcely have been unaware of the appearance of this volume; nor, in view of his recent visit to Russia and his intention of writing on the subject at an early date, could he have been uninterested in it. And indeed, a glance at this work, alongside that of Custine, strongly suggests such a relationship. The similarity will be found not so much in individual passages, although there are one or two striking instances of this nature, but rather in the spirit of the two works and in the frequent identity of theme. The sense of vast distance; the dreariness and endlessness of the Russian roads; the sinister figure of the Tsarist courier —the *feldjaeger*—flaunting his brutal authority over lesser folk;† the monotony of the village houses; the pretentious-

---

* The likelihood that Mickiewicz' poem received Custine's attention seems to me to be enhanced by the fact that Ostrowski, the Polish translator, later appeared among the approving critics of Custine's book.

† Note, for example:

From Mickiewicz's *Digression*:	From *La Russie en 1839*:
Now a kibitka suddenly flies by: The ambulances, guns, and guards who ride, Rush madly from the road as it comes nigh; Even the leaders' wagons draw aside. Still on and on it flies: the gendarme whacks	"A little further on I saw a mounted courier, a *feldjaeger* or some other infamous employee of the government, get out of his carriage, run up to one of the two polite coachmen and strike him brutally with his whip, with a stick, and with his fists. . . ." (3rd edition, II, 200)

ness and imitativeness of Petersburg; the exorbitant cost of
the creation of that city; the historical predominance of the
ruthless, heavy-handed figure of Peter the Great as symbolized by his ponderous equestrian statue in Petersburg;
the image of Petersburg as a city created by fiat of this
single ruler rather than by natural historical development;
the degradation of the Russian Orthodox Church through
its domination by the Tsarist bureaucracy; the humiliating
obsequiousness of the nobility and the courtiers—all these
themes, and others, will be found common to the two works.

It must be emphasized, however, that if, as we may pre-
sume to have been the case, Custine became acquainted
with Mickiewicz' *Digression,* he did so only *after* completion of his own journey to Russia. He must have recognized in Mickiewicz' lines many impressions which he, a
sensitive, intelligent, and critically-inclined traveller, had
already gained from his own experience. Mickiewicz' poem
can thus have served him primarily, and probably did, only
as a reminder of themes to be treated; it is not likely to
have provided the substance for any of his observations.

The driver with his fist; the
driver thwacks
The soldiers with his whip; the
throng gives way;
The wheels crush anyone who
dares to stay. Whither?—Who
rides within?—
No one will ask.
The gendarme speeds on some
important task:
Surely he rides on orders from
the tsar.
"Perhaps that gendarme travels
from afar."
A general suggests. . . .
(Quoted in Wacław Lednicki,
*Pushkin's Bronze Horseman.
The Story of a Masterpiece,*
Berkeley and Los Angeles,
University of California Press,
1955, p., 112)

And again—about the *feldjaeger:*
"The *feldjaeger* is the man of
power; he is the word of the master; he is a living telegraph line.
Those of them whom I see . . .
represent for me the solitudes
into which they are about to
plunge. I follow them in imagination at the end of their route:
Siberia, Kamchatka, the saline
desert. . . ."
(*Ibid.,* II, 87-88)

III. *CUSTINE'S*
"ROAD TO RUSSIA"

CUSTINE appears to have left Paris, accompanied by his Italian manservant, Antonio, and Gurowski, in late May, 1839. Well over a month was to pass before he would take ship for Kronstadt at Travemünde. Some uncertainty surrounds his movements during that period. He himself was obviously at pains to distort the record with relation to certain of them; and this places in question the accuracy of his statements about all the others. The following itinerary and chronology may be taken, however, as approximately accurate.

By June 3, Custine and Gurowski were at Bad Ems, in the Rhineland. It was not by accident, surely, that their arrival was followed shortly by that of the heir to the Russian throne, the Grand Duke Alexander Nikolayevich. Custine names this event as the real beginning of his Russian voyage. He witnessed personally the arrival of the Grand Duke, and began his book with the description of it. He saw the Grand Duke again, he says, the following day, and amplified, on the basis of this second experience, his description of him, noting in him, among other things, a rather frightening capacity for dissimulation—a quality which, he adds cynically, revealed the prince as one indeed destined to exercise great power. What he does not relate in his account is that he took the occasion to present Gurowski to the Grand Duke, thus inaugurating his effort on the young man's behalf.

On or about June 8 Custine (probably no longer accompanied by Gurowski) left Ems and proceeded to Frankfurt. Here he evidently stopped for about a fortnight. He then moved on to Bad Kissingen, some sixty-five miles further east, where he arrived about June 24. (In pursuing this route, he was, incidentally, following the Grand Duke, who appears to have arrived at Kissingen on the 18th.) Custine spent only a day or two at Kissingen, and then pressed on to Berlin. Here, too, he could have stopped only a very short time, for by July 3 he was already at Lübeck, preparing to embark from the nearby Travemünde.

It must be noted that Custine, in the account of this journey that appears in his book, says nothing of his visits to Frankfurt or to Bad Kissingen. On the contrary, he gives the impression that he proceeded directly from Ems to Berlin. To reinforce this impression he even falsifies the date of his arrival in the latter place. One is naturally moved to curiosity concerning the reasons for this distortion.

While at Bad Kissingen (and possibly also at Frankfurt, for the two were evidently proceeding along the same route), Custine met a Russian acquaintance, a man whom he had long known in Paris, and received from him a letter of introduction to certain other people in Russia. The Russian acquaintance in question was a man well-known in the history of Russian letters: Alexander Ivanovich Turgenev.

Elder cousin of the great novelist Ivan Sergeyevich Turgenev, Alexander Ivanovich was one of four sons of the second director of Moscow University, Ivan Petrovich Turgenev—one of the most erudite men in the Russia of his time. After undergoing a tour of training in the Foreign Office Archives in his younger years, Alexander entered governmental service and served variously, during the reign of Alexander I, as a director in the Department of Ecclesiastical Affairs, as a staff official in the Council of State, and as a member of the staff of the Legislative Commission. After the Decembrist insurrection he appears to have resided, for a complex of personal and political reasons, mostly abroad. He found a task that evidently suited him from both the personal and political point of view: the task, that is, of unearthing from the official archives of various European governments historical materials on Russia generally and on the relations between respective governments and the Russian government in particular. This gave him the possibility of living for years on end in Western Europe. He made Paris his headquarters, and it was there that he was spending much of his time in the late 1830's.

A stout, breathless man, ever on the move—a man profoundly social in his tastes and habits—a congenital bachelor, enjoying that special freedom and mobility of social life that so often goes with the celibate state: Alexander Turgenev was a stupendous, but talented and amiable, busybody. To this calling he devoted energies of formidable dimensions. He knew everyone in the social and literary worlds of France and Russia. He was a warm and generous friend to dozens of literati in both countries. He was an indefatigable letter-writer. His letters, surviving by the thousands into later decades, have been published in various historical series*; and they form one of the great funds of source material for the history of Russian literature in the first decades of the nineteenth century. Aside from scurrying frequently back and forth personally between Russia and France, he made of himself, with the help of his most intimate friends in Russia, and particularly A. Ya. Bulgakov, Postmaster at Moscow, and Prince P. A. Vyazemski (see below), a veritable post office for the exchange of

* Many hundreds of these letters—the ones addressed to Vyazemski or members of his family—will be found in the *Ostaf 'evski Arkhiv Knyazei Vyazemskikh*, the collection of papers taken from the Vyazemski family estate of Ostaf'evo and published in several volumes, in St. Petersburg, over the years 1899 to 1913. Many others, from the earlier period of Turgenev's life, are included in the series entitled *Arkhiv Brat'ev Turgenevykh*, Petrograd, Izdanie Otdeleniya Russkogo Yazyka i Slovesnosti Akademii Nauk, 1911-1921. A voluminous collection of letters to the Bulgakov brothers was published in 1939 by the Moscow Lenin Library, under the title of *Pis'ma Aleksandra Turgeneva Bulgakovym*. Further collections have been published, at one time or another, in Russian historical serials.

literary materials between Russia and France. His correspondence is replete with references to the packages of
printed matter he was constantly sending from one of these
countries to the other. He functioned in Paris, in fact, as
a species of informal cultural attaché.

Turgenev's relations with the regime of Nicholas I were
complicated. His background was that of the liberal-aristo-
cratic intelligentsia of the period of Alexander I, for whom
the adjustment to the regime of Nicholas was always difficult and often painful. His well-known brother Nikolai,
also a writer of note, had been involved in the Decembrist
conspiracy, but had happened to be abroad at the time of
the insurrection, and was obliged to live for decades thereafter as an exile in Western Europe. Alexander not only remained devoted to this politically-compromised brother, but
appeared to share in large degree the liberal impulses—the
unhappiness over the outcome of the Decembrist affair
and the suppression of the Polish uprising, and the general
resentment of the heavy-handed oppressiveness of the
Nikolayevan regime—that were felt by so many of his
friends. That he was not always entirely secure in his foreign residence is suggested by a reference, in one of his
letters, to a reassurance he had received privately from some
high Petersburg quarter that he need fear no adverse reaction to his continuing to reside abroad for at least another
year or so. And while it would be wrong to view his historical-archival work in Western Europe as perfunctory, or
as a mere pretext for getting out of Russia, one cannot
avoid the impression that this function also served as a
welcome means of justifying a prolonged absence from
Russia in a difficult time, enabling him to avoid certain
problems of conscience which, for anyone of his views and
connections, life in Russia would inevitably have posed.
One gains, from his correspondence, the impression of a
highly cultured man, of liberal views, in passive if not
active political opposition to the regime of Nicholas I,
living in Paris as a means of avoiding the oppressive atmosphere of the Russia of the day, and using his foreign resi-

dence plus his excellent personal connections as a means of keeping his friends in Russia abreast of cultural and literary trends in Western Europe.

Yet we must also note that Turgenev had good connections in Russian officialdom and does not appear, at this stage of his life, to have been in any way in disfavor with the Russian government. While his academic work appears to have been done on behalf of the Russian government—particularly the Ministry of Education, which published the results of it, I have no evidence that he was considered a government official.* But his relations with the Russian diplomatic missions in Paris and elsewhere were, in at least some instances, close and cordial. Much of his voluminous personal correspondence went through official channels, where it could hardly have been immune from scrutiny by various curious and critical official eyes. Not only this, but he seems to have been personally, and not unfavorably, known to the Emperor. He had, after all, been a close personal friend of Pushkin. He had been in attendance on the poet throughout the long hours of death agony following the duel in 1836. He had been one of the few persons present at the bedside when the poet died. He had then been selected, either at the initiative of the Emperor or with the latter's carefully-considered approval, as the sole person, aside from one officer of the gendarmerie, charged with the task of escorting the body on the last weird journey, by sleigh, to its final resting place near Pskov. Considering the Tsar's painful personal interest in Pushkin, and particularly in the episode of his death and burial, this would seem to have been very much a mark of confidence.

* He seems occasionally to have been referred to by others by his official title of "State Secretary"; but this, I believe, was a title which continued to be borne by the holder even when he was not in active service.

The materials Turgenev collected were published in 1841-42 by the Archaeological Commission of the Russian Ministry of Education, under the Russian title, *Akty istoricheskie, otnosyashchiesya do Rossii, izvlechennye iz inostrannykh arkhivov i bibliotek A. I. Turgenevym,* and a corresponding Latin title, *Historica Russiae Monumenta ex antiquis exterarum gentium archivis deprompta ab A. J. Turgenevio,* 1841.

Custine in 1846, aquarelle by the Comtesse de Menou

LA RUSSIE

EN 1839

PAR

LE MARQUIS DE CUSTINE

« Respectez surtout les étrangers, de quelque qualité, de quelque
« rang qu'ils soient, et si vous n'êtes pas à même de les combler
« de présents , prodiguez-leur au moins des marques de bienveil-
« lance , puisque de la manière dont ils sont traités dans un pays
« dépend le bien et le mal qu'ils en disent en retournant dans
« le leur. »

Extrait des conseils de Vladimir Monomaque à ses enfants en 1126
Histoire de l'Empire de Russie , par Karamsin , t. II , p. 205)

TOME PREMIER

PARIS

LIBRAIRIE D'AMYOT, ÉDITEUR

6, RUE DE LA PAIX

1843

Title page of the first edition

The recommendation which Turgenev gave to Custine at Kissingen, on June 25, was actually only part of a letter of that date from Turgenev to his close friend at Petersburg, the poet and critic Prince Pyotr Andreyevich Vyazemski—a letter which Custine was asked to take with him and to deliver to Vyazemski upon arrival in Petersburg. It contained the following passage:

> The Marquis de Custine, author of . . . , will bring you this letter together with another one from the princess [Vyazemski's wife]. He is a friend of Chateaubriand and of *la Récamier*; you met him at her house. Recommend him to Prince Odoyevski from myself and from Varnhagen, who is closely connected with him. He knew his [Varnhagen's] wife, Rahel. . . . He writes accounts of his journeys. If he goes to Moscow, send him to Bulgakov and to Chaadayev on my behalf, and to Sverbeyeva—for the honor to Russian beauty.[1]

Just how much importance to assign to this letter from the standpoint of the background of Custine's journey and the inspiration of his views is a question for which existing evidence still permits of no firm answer—possibly not very much; but since Custine had discussions about Russian questions with at least one and probably most of these people, since there are certain intriguing mysteries that still surround their relations with one another and their connection with his journey, and since the similarity of Custine's views to those of one of them—Chaadayev—has sometimes been noted even by scholars to whom the existence of this letter was unknown, it becomes necessary to have a closer look at their identity.

Prince Petr Andreyevich Vyazemski, well-known critic, poet, and life-long intimate friend of Turgenev, was a man of high distinction in the literary life of that day. He had been if not the closest, one of the very closest of Pushkin's friends. His own works were known for their biting, satirical quality—a quality often employed, in his younger years, for veiled attacks on the government. His greatest genius was unquestionably the critical one.

After serving as an officer in the War of 1812 (he fought at Borodino) and then for a time as an aide to the Viceroy in Poland, Vyazemski, like many others, became disillusioned and estranged from the government during the final years of the reign of Alexander I. He barely missed involvement in the Decembrist affair. He later made his peace with the regime of Nicholas, but only at the cost of re-entering governmental service—this time, the service of the Ministry of Finance. Here, with the course of the years, he learned gradually to take an interest in his official duties, but became progressively more bitter and defensive (particularly with relation to his own past), more conservative, and more inclined to defend the regime in the face of foreign critics. At the time of Custine's visit he was serving as Deputy Director for Foreign Trade, under the Ministry of Finance.

In the preceding winter he had received from the Russian government permission to visit Germany for treatment to his eyes; and he had availed himself of this occasion for paying a visit to Paris as well, where, despite a perfect knowledge of French and the enjoyment of many ties with French people, he had never been. To the disappointment of his friend Turgenev, who served as his guide and introducer in French society, Vyazemski did not enjoy the experience, and came away from it, by all accounts, bored and disappointed. It was during this visit to Paris that he had met Custine (very casually, one must assume) *chez* Madame Récamier.

Vyazemski, one might note, had received a good portion of his education in a Jesuit *pension* in Moscow. During his early service in Poland he had conceived a strong interest in, and some sympathy for, the Poles—a disposition which had no doubt been strengthened by close friendship with Mickiewicz, some of whose sonnets he had translated into Russian. One can imagine that by the late thirties, Pushkin now being dead, Mickiewicz an exile in Paris, and the memory of the intervening Polish uprising still rankling in everyone's mind, Poland was—for Vyazemski—a most sensitive and painful subject. His memories and connections from earlier times, including his Catholic education, must have made it difficult for him to approve his government's action towards Poland. His friendship with Pushkin, his growing conservatism and his reconciliation with the regime must, on the other hand, have made it equally difficult for him to condemn it.

Prince Vladimir Fedorovich Odoyevski—the first of those to whom Vyazemski was asked to pass Custine along —was a well-known man in Petersburg: a writer, an editor, an aesthete, and a musicologist of note. While not a man of great wealth, he was known for his hospitality. One reads of other French writers (Marmier and the young playwright Auger are two) being taken to see him, in just those years; and one wonders whether his distinction as a cultural figure and his generosity as a host were not exploited by the government or by his friends, or both, as a means of accommodating foreign visitors to whom it was desired that Petersburg should show a friendly and attractive face.

A. Ya. Bulgakov was the Postmaster at Moscow. He was an old and close friend of Turgenev and Vyazemski. He had been a diplomat in his younger days. His assumption of the position of postmaster had apparently served, as did Vyazemski's acceptance of the position with the Ministry of Finance, as a means of regularizing his relationship to the regime of Nicholas I. (His brother Konstantin, who died in 1835, had been Director General of the Russian postal service.) Bulgakov's position was also useful to his friends—for purposes both of transportation and communication. It placed him in control of the postal stations and the relays of postal horses which constituted, in this period just preceding the building of railways, the principal mode of travel for private persons of means. This, together with his control over the mails, enabled him to render valuable service to Turgenev—certainly in the rapid transmission of the latter's innumerable letters and parcels and perhaps also in their protection from the delays and embarrassments of the censorship. What between Vyazemski's presence in the

Department of Foreign Trade, where he was in a position to use his influence with the customs, and Alexander Bulgakov's control of the postal service at Moscow, Turgenev had excellent facilities for the expedition of his voluminous correspondence. Aside from the question as to whether Bulgakov had any intellectual influence on Custine, there can be no doubt that it was through his authority that Custine was provided with the horse-relays and other facilities for his journey from Moscow to Nizhni Novgorod and return.

The second person in Moscow to whom Vyazemski was asked to recommend Custine was one whose name is familiar to every student of Russian history and literature. This was none other than the religious philosopher, eccentric, and author of the famous *Philosophic Letter*, Pyotr Yakovlevich Chaadayev.

Chaadayev was perhaps the most striking example of those talented, frustrated, and embittered noblemen who, though enjoying close personal and intellectual relations with the Decembrists, had in one way or another escaped direct complicity in the conspiracy and had survived to accommodate themselves as best they could to the bitter realities of the period of Nicholas I. (They have sometimes been termed—and not unaptly—"Decembrists without December.") Spending as he did the remainder of his life in retirement and isolation in Moscow, dominating Moscow society, whenever he appeared in it, by his intellectual ascendancy, his proud, romantic aloofness, and his impressive eloquence, Chaadayev seems to me (there are differing opinions about this) to have been the obvious prototype for the hero of Griboyedov's great play *Gore ot Uma* (*Sorrow from Wit*).

To understand the interest that has often been shown in the possible connection between Chaadayev's thought and Custine's book, it is necessary to bear in mind the nature and general tenor of the *Philosophic Letter*. This term is usually taken to refer to the first of a series of documents written privately by Chaadayev in 1829 and intended as the expression of his views on a number of great problems of religious and political philosophy, including particularly his interpretation of the role of religion in the past history and the future destinies of the Russian state.* Copies of this first letter, in particular, were handed about among Chaadayev's friends in the early 1830's—some time before it appeared in published form. They even reached Paris, through the agency of none other than Alexander Turgenev, and were circulated there among a number of Turgenev's French acquaintances. Having been written in French (in which language Chaadayev was more at home than in his native Russian), they required no translation for French readers.

It will be recalled that in the mid-1830's, this first "philosophic letter" suddenly saw publication in Russian translation (not at Chaadayev's initiative, though also not without his tacit approval) in one of the Russian literary journals, the *Teleskop*. The sequel is well known. The Tsar, infuriated, caused Chaadayev to be declared officially of unsound mind, to be placed under virtual house-arrest, and to be visited daily, for many months thereafter, by a military physician.

The *Philosophic Letter* has now of course become famous in the annals of Russian literature and Russian religious-political thought. Chaadayev's biographer and interpreter, Gershenzon, writing in the first years of this present century, pointed out that it had almost invariably been read and judged out of context, and that the result was widespread popular misconception concerning the true nature of Chaadayev's ideas. This is no doubt true. It was probably true even in the 1830's. But since it would have been by this popular misconception, derived from the one famous letter, rather than by any scholarly scrutiny of the man's entire life and work, that Custine would have been influenced, if he was influenced by Chaadayev at all, we are safe in

---

* Only the first of these documents was published in Chaadayev's time. Some of the others were not unearthed until the present century, and only recently were the original French texts published for the first time (see Raymond T. McNally, *Chaadayev's Philosophical Letters*, Wiesbaden, Forschungen zur osteuropäischen Geschichte, Vol. 11, Berlin, 1966).

taking this letter as a standard of comparison with Custine's work. And such comparison suggests that the similarity exists not so much in point of content as in tone. It is Chaadayev's sorrowful cadences, constituting as they did a sort of lyrical lament for Russia—her unhappy history, her wasted opportunities, her underdevelopment, the futility in the lives of her gifted people—that suggest most strongly the negative quality of Custine's subsequent work.*

It remains to be noted that Chaadayev, though not actually a Roman Catholic, was often reputed or suspected

---

* There are many passages of the *Philosophic Letter* that might be cited to illustrate this point. The following will do, perhaps, as well as any:

But I ask you: where do you find our sages, where do you find our thinkers? Who has ever done any thinking on our behalf, who thinks on our behalf today? And yet, placed as we are between the two great divisions of the world, between the Orient and the West, touching at one end on China and at the other on Germany, we ought to have united in ourselves the two great principles of intelligent nature: imagination and reason, and in this way united within our civilization the histories of the entire globe. But this is not at all the role that Providence has allotted to us. Far from it: Providence does not seem to have occupied itself with our fate at all. It has left us wholly to our own devices; it has not wished to be involved with us; it has had nothing to teach us. The experience of the ages is as nothing for us; the ages and the generations have glided away from us without result. One would say, to look at us, that the general law of humanity had been revoked in our case. Solitary *in* the world, we have given nothing *to* the world, we have learned nothing *from* the world; we have not added a single idea to the totality of human ideas; we have contributed nothing to the human spirit; and all that has come to us of its progress we have disfigured. Nothing, from the very first instant of our social existence, has come out of us for the good of humanity; not a single thought has germinated in the sterile soil of our fatherland; not a single great truth has emerged from our midst; we have not even given ourselves the trouble to imagine anything; and of all that others have imagined we have borrowed nothing but deceptive appearances and useless luxury. . . .

We grow, but we do not mature. We advance, but only obliquely, along a line that does not lead us to our goal. We are like infants . . . whose entire knowledge is on the surface of their being, whose entire soul is outside themselves. . . .

To make ourselves noticed in the world, we would have to expand from Bering Sea to the Oder.[2]

to be one, and that his view of the western church was indeed much more tolerant and sympathetic than the one that was common to educated Russians of that day.

The last of the people to whom Custine was recommended, Katerina Alexandrovna Sverbeyeva, is of little importance from the standpoint of this discussion. Her husband, Dmitri Nikolayevich Sverbeyev, was an old friend of Chaadayev, and she herself a distant relative. She conducted in Moscow a salon patronized by many prominent Moscow figures, including Chaadayev. In contrast to the other persons mentioned in Turgenev's letter, Vyazemski was asked to send Custine to her not on Turgenev's behalf but "for the honor to Russian beauty"—a rather strange idea, actually, considering what Turgenev must have known of Custine's preferences in the matter of personal beauty.

It was, then, with this letter of introduction in his pocket that Custine, at the end of June, 1839, made his way, via Berlin, to Lübeck, where he stopped for a night or two before embarking, at Travemünde, on the steamer for Kronstadt. This steamer connection, served at the time by a vessel of combined sail and paddle-wheel propulsion called the *Nicholas I*, had been in existence for some years, through the summer season, at least; and it had, despite one disaster of the previous season when the steamer caught fire off the coast of the Isle of Rügen, attained a considerable popularity with upper-class Russians as a relatively quick and easy means of passage between St. Petersburg and western Europe.

The inn at which Custine stopped, at Lübeck, was thus one much patronized by Russian travellers; and it was from his brief sojourn there that he derived what became one of the most famous passages of his book. The innkeeper, with whom he fell into conversation, expressed wonder that Custine should wish to go to Russia. Custine asked why this should be a source of surprise to him. The innkeeper then explained that his Russian guests seemed to have two physiognomies. "When they leave the ship on their way to Europe," he said, "they have a gay, free, happy air about them; they are like escaped horses, like birds out of the cage, men, women, young, and old: all are happy as students on a holiday; but the same persons, on their return, are drooping, sombre, tormented figures, preoccupied, taciturn, with worried faces. . . ."[3]

No passage, incidentally, stung the Tsar's regime more painfully than this one. Not one of the semi-official Russian critics who set out, after the book's appearance, to attack and refute Custine's conclusions, failed to insist that the reason the Russians were all so happy when they left the ship on arrival in Germany was that they had been deathly seasick on board and were glad to be back on dry land, whereas their gloom as they passed through Lübeck on return arose from the dread of a new maritime ordeal.

Shortly after boarding the ship at Travemünde, and while waiting for the vessel to sail, Custine witnessed the laborious arrival of a fellow-passenger, a Russian prince, a man so obese and infirm that he had to be assisted on board. The two men soon fell into the first of a series of conversations, the detailed record of which was later to occupy a prominent place in Custine's book. The prince, with whose personality and discourse Custine was utterly charmed, proceeded during the course of the voyage to give Custine a small lecture course on the history of Russia, on the differences between Russia's historical development and that of the West, on the contemporary features of Russian government, and particularly on the relations, in Russia, of Church and State. What emerged from these statements was not at all a chauvinistic Russian view; on the contrary, it was a very western, very detached, and—with relation to Russia itself—deeply skeptical and pessimistic one. It might be summarized, in paraphrase, as follows:

> Russia was separated by scarcely four hundred years from the barbarian invasions, whereas it was fourteen hundred years since the West had gone through this crisis; such a difference in age made a tremendous difference in the customs of nations.

Russia, long before the Tatar invasion, had received its rulers from Scandinavia; and these had received in turn their tastes, their arts, and their luxuries from the emperors and patriarchs of Constantinople.

Brilliant figures of saints and rulers, and sometimes combinations of the two, had flashed across the dark skies of medieval Russia; but these did not resemble the great men of the West. They were less like men of the age of chivalry than like Biblical kings, who had retained their patriarchal customs. The Russians, accordingly, had not been brought up in that school of good faith that shaped the chivalresque traditions of medieval Europe. They knew the concept neither of "honor" nor of "word of honor." The spread of that spirit of chivalry towards the East might be said to have stopped with Poland. The Poles had fought romantically—for the sake of glory. The Russians were also warriors—but they fought only for the sake of conquest. They were governed, as warriors, by obedience and greed. A chasm had therefore grown up between these two Slavic nations—Poland and Russia—which it would take centuries to overcome.

While Europe was still panting from its efforts to recover the tomb of Christ from the power of miscreants, the Russians were paying tribute to the Moslems and continuing to receive from the Byzantine Empire their habits, arts, customs, sciences, religion, their aversion to the Latin crusades, and their political life, with all its addiction to ruses and frauds.

Russian despotism, as known in the xix century, had been founded at the very moment when slavery was being abolished in the rest of Europe. Since the invasion by the Mongols, the Slavs, once among the freest of peoples, had become the slaves—first of their Asian conquerors, then of their own princes; and this had degraded the entire tenor of Russian public life.[4]

Particularly striking were the Prince's observations on the connection between religion and politics in the policies of the Russian government. "Don't think," the Prince said to Custine (and this time I quote verbatim Custine's version of his words),

> that the persecution of Poland is the product of personal *ressentiment* on the part of the Emperor: it is the result of cold and profound calculation. These acts of cruelty are meritorious in the eyes of true believers. It is the Holy Ghost who enlightens the sovereign to the point of elevating his soul above any and every humane sentiment, and God gives his blessing to the executor of his high purposes. Looked at in this way, judges and hangmen are all the more saintly the more barbaric they are. Your legitimist newspapers don't know what they are talking about when they seek allies among the Schismatics. We will sooner see a European revolution than we will see the Emperor of Russia serve a Catholic party in good faith. It would be easier to reunite the Protestants to the Papacy than to do the same with the head of the Russian autocracy, because the Protestants . . . have nothing but their sectarian pride to sacrifice to Rome, whereas the Emperor possesses a very real and very positive spiritual power of which he will never divest himself voluntarily. Rome and all that attaches to the Roman Church has no enemies more dangerous than the autocrat of Moscow, visible head of his own church; and I am amazed that the native perspicacity of the Italians has thus far failed to detect the danger that menaces us from that quarter.[5]

These statements, as will readily be seen, were ones of a militant Catholicism, sharply antagonistic both to the Russian crown and to the Russian Church. And the prominence which Custine accords to them in his account testifies to the deep impression they made upon him.

Custine, in writing his book, was at pains (though not *excessive* pains) to conceal the identity of this extraordinary interlocutor, referring to him only as "Prince K***." Actually, the man's identity is unmistakable, and his personality deserves, both for its own sake and because of its importance for Custine's journey, a closer scrutiny.

Prince Pyotr Borisovich Kozlovski had started his career, at the turn of the century, as a Russian diplomat. He had been Russian Chargé d'Affaires at the court of Sardinia at the time when Joseph de Maistre was Sardinian Chargé in Petersburg. He, like Custine, had been at the Congress of Vienna. In 1820, he had left the diplomatic service, reputedly because he insisted on filing a report, dealing with Metternich's policy towards Germany, which went contrary to the views of the Emperor.* Instead of returning at once to Russia, however, he continued for many years to live in Western Europe as a private citizen. He returned to Russia only in 1835, after an unbroken absence of twenty-three years. He then collaborated for a time with Pushkin as a contributor to the latter's literary journal, the *Sovremennik*. In 1836 or thereabouts, he was re-accepted into Russian governmental service and sent to Warsaw to serve as an aide to the Viceroy there, Marshal Paskevich. This he did for some three years, specializing, at the Marshal's orders, on educational problems and devising an extensive and successful program for the integration of the Polish secondary schools into the Russian school system.† Whether his service in Warsaw had been terminated at this point, or whether he was merely going on leave of absence, is not

* It is not to be excluded that Kozlovski's retirement was in part, at least, the product of Metternich's influence.

† References to Kozlovski's service in Warsaw will be found in the biography of Paskevich by Prince Shcherbatov entitled: *General fel'dmarshal Knyaz Paskevich. Ego zhizn'i dyeatel'nost*, Petersburg, 1896, Vol. V. Shcherbatov refers to Kozlovski as "an old, excellently educated and intelligent diplomat . . . to whom the Tsar was not well-disposed but who lived in the residence of the Prince of Warsaw [i.e., Paskevich] as a friend of the family and was officially assigned to him as an aide for special purposes." While the Marshal obviously liked Kozlovski and appreciated his unusual qualities of mind, it is a depressing reflection of the atmosphere of the Russian bureaucracy of the reign of Nicholas I that he caused Kozlovski, even while the latter was a guest in his own house, to be shadowed by the Russian secret police. This may, however, have been done for Kozlovski's own protection.

clear. He was, in any case, at the time of his meeting with Custine, on his way back to Russia; and it was to be one of his last journeys. He was destined to die in Germany the following year—a circumstance which alone permitted Custine to quote him as liberally and effectively as he did in the expression of sentiments that would certainly, had Kozlovski been alive, have heightened greatly the Emperor's long-standing suspicion of him.

Kozlovski was a man fabulous, rather than famous, in many of the diplomatic and social salons of the Europe of his day—fabulous for his great girth, for his facial resemblance to the Bourbons (particularly Louis XVI), for his warm, generous personality, and above all for his exceptional brilliance, wit, and charm as a conversationalist. His was indeed a tragic personality—a bit that of the physically-slothful intellectual, a bit that of the Falstaff. One suspects that a feeling for good grace reduced him on many occasions (as it has many other fat people) to playing the clown, as the easiest way of appearing to share the amusement induced in others by the sight of his great bulk. But those who knew him were unanimous in the recognition that behind all this there lay a mind of great seriousness and originality. People adored to hear him talk. Parties were arranged around his presence, as though for some great musician who had agreed to play. It is said that on one occasion he even spoke aloud in installments, to a group of his friends, an entire novel which he had in his head but was too lazy to write down. I am indebted to the Oxford Slavist, John Simmons, for the information that Kozlovski was the first Russian ever to receive an honorary degree at Oxford, preceding in this honor even the Tsar Alexander I.* This could have been, I think, only a tribute to such of his qualities as were manifested in his conversation, for he seldom wrote anything. The miserable letters of the alphabet, he claimed, interfered with the even flow of his thoughts.

* See J.S.G. Simmons, "Turgenev and Oxford," *Oxoniensia*, xxxi (1966), 146.

Kozlovski was in the deepest sense of the term an expatriate. Most of his adult and professional life had been spent outside of Russia. It was with good reason that Professor Gleb Struve gave to the account of his life the title *Russki Evropeyets—A Russian European.** Kozlovski's closest personal ties were in Europe. He was leaving behind him, on this last trip to Russia, a sort of morganatic Italian wife, and two children.† Not only this, but he was (and this is particularly significant for his influence on Custine) unquestionably a Roman Catholic—not in the sense that he had become a pious Catholic churchgoer, but rather that he had formed a belief in the justice and legitimacy of the claim of the Roman See to a universal pastorship, and was, as such, of course an opponent of the pretensions of Eastern Orthodoxy, including those of the Russian Orthodox Church. All this had naturally strengthened his bond with the Poles, and it presumably added great weight to his judgments in the eyes of Custine.

During the period of his service in Warsaw, Kozlovski was known as a good friend of the Poles, on whose behalf he is said to have interceded on many occasions with the Viceroy. It is interesting to note in this connection the speculations that have been entertained concerning the identity of the object of a fragment of a poem composed by Pushkin, evidently in 1834 or 1835, but discovered and brought to light only at the beginning of this century. In these incomplete verses the poet bitterly criticized some unnamed person for tenderly loving foreign peoples while he hated his own and, in particular, for rubbing his hands in pleasure over the Russian reverses at the time of the Polish uprising

---

* San Francisco: Publishing House "Delo," 1950. For such knowledge as I have of the life and personality of Kozlovski, I am indebted almost exclusively to this valuable brief biography published by Professor Struve, of the University of California. Professor Struve has done a signal service to Russian political and literary history by resurrecting this interesting historical figure from the oblivion that might well otherwise have eventually obscured it entirely.

† It is one of the many curious and peripheral circumstances that seem to bind together the main characters of this account that the daughter eventually became another of Balzac's admired ladies.

of 1830-31. The late Professor Wacław Lednicki was inclined to the view that these verses were directed against
either Chaadayev or Vyazemski. Professor Struve, in his
work on Kozlovski mentioned above, has argued convinc-
ingly that a much more likely target for the reproaches was
Kozlovski. He, in contrast to Chaadayev, was indeed known
to have entertained strong sympathies for the Poles at the
time of the uprising. And in contrast to Vyazemski, he was
indeed an expatriate, extensively alienated from the society
of his own country. It will suffice for us to note, at this
point, that all three of these men were closely connected
with Custine's journey.

Had Custine's account really represented all that there
was to say about his relationship with Kozlovski and about
the latter's connection with other circumstances of his journey, we could leave this colorful and impressive individual
at this point. But here, again, there are certain curious circumstances that have to be noted, even if there are no
adequate answers to the questions they raise.

Kozlovski, in the first place, turns out to be by no means
unrelated to the various persons mentioned in Turgenev's
letter of introduction. On the contrary, one learns from
Professor Struve's book that Alexander Turgenev, Alexander's brother Nikolai, and the two Bulgakov brothers, were
Kozlovski's oldest and most intimate friends, and that with
Vyazemski, too, albeit at a later date, he had formed a close
and warm relationship. It was Turgenev and Vyazemski
who wrote, the following year, the memorial tributes published on the occasion of his death.

But secondly there is the fact that whereas Custine leaves
with his readers the impression that he met Kozlovski for
the first time on board the ship and was obliged to inquire
of others to ascertain his identity, there is strong evidence
that this was not so: that, on the contrary, the two men had
actually met only shortly before, during Custine's stop at
Frankfurt in June; and that it was there, and not on the
ship, that at least a portion of those discussions between

them took place which Custine reports in his book.* Why, one wonders, all this secrecy and evasion? Kozlovski, at the time the book was completed for publication, had been dead and gone those three years. Nothing could any longer have hurt *him*. Why, then, should Custine have gone to the trouble of disguising their prior acquaintance and their recent meeting in Frankfurt? This question remains, for the moment, without answer.

Individual fates seem indeed to have been strangely entangled in those days. There was at least one other passenger on board the *Nicholas I* who was destined later to play a part, albeit a minor and not wholly serious one, in relation to Custine's book. This was a man whom Custine thought to recognize—and correctly so, as the historical record now confirms—as a Russian spy, curious to learn about the purposes of his journey and to draw him out in his views about Russia. Custine ticked him off, mercilessly, three years later, in the pages of his book. He was approached on shipboard, he recounted, by

> une espèce de savant russe, un grammairien, traducteur de plusieurs ouvrages allemands, professeur à je ne sais quel collège. . . . La liberté de ses discours m'a paru suspecte. . . . J'ai pensé qu'il devait toujours

* Custine would appear to have arrived in Frankfurt June 9 or 10. Alexander Turgenev's correspondence indicates that he, Turgenev, met Kozlovski there on the 8th. The fine scholarly eye of M. Cadot has noted that at the end of several passages of Custine's reflections, described as having been induced by Kozlovski's observations, there is a cryptic little footnote (p. 150 of Vol. I in the 3rd edition) to the effect that these passages were actually written on June 10, 1839. M. Cadot also noticed that the phrase indicating that the meeting on the ship was the first encounter between the two men did not appear in the first edition but was introduced only in the second and succeeding ones.
It should be noted that one of Custine's oldest and closest friends in Frankfurt was Varnhagen von Ense, who was also a close friend of Kozlovski. All three had been at the Congress of Vienna, many years before. It would be very natural, therefore, that Custine should have met Kozlovski, when in Frankfurt.

se rencontrer quelque savant de cette espèce aux ap-
proches de la Russie . . . son inquiétude, que j'ai su
calmer, a éveillé la mienne.[6]

This episode has its amusing side, for the gentleman in
question, stung, no doubt, by these biting words, later re-
venged himself by taking his place among the most bitter
public critics of Custine's book. He was indeed a grammarian, and in fact a well-known literary figure: Nikolai
Ivanovich Grech, journalist, editor, author of a book of
some lasting value on the grammar and structure of the
Russian language. He appears to have spent much of his
time, just in those years, in Paris. He did indeed serve the
Russian police from time to time as a source of information
on the Russian colony there. He was, however, not noted
for his discretion, and his zeal as an informer was not less
visible to others than it was to Custine. The Paris Poles are
said to have taken pleasure, at one point, in distributing
around Paris spurious visiting cards bearing the inscrip-
tion: "N. Gretsch, Grand Espion de Sa Majesté l'Empereur
de Russie."*

Before leaving the account of Custine's approach to the
Russian scene, it will be well to turn once more to those
others, already mentioned in this chapter, whose relationship to Custine's journey was a more serious one than that
of Grech, and to recall something of the climate of opinion
by which, at that time, such men as Kozlovski and Turgenev and the ones mentioned in Turgenev's letter were surrounded.

---

* It would be easy, from this brief description, to underrate Grech
as a literary person and to exaggerate the importance of his services
to the Russian police. If he served as a source of information for the
latter, and if he even sought financial rewards for these services, as
he seems occasionally to have done, he viewed this activity primarily
as a form of service to the Emperor, and can be blamed, if he is to
be blamed at all, more for sycophancy than for sinister intent. The
police, well aware of the narrow limits of his discretion, tended to
deal with him prudently, and at arm's length. His well-written but
unfinished autobiography (*Zapiski o moei zhizni*, Petersburg, 1856)
is another major source for the literary history of his time.

Prince Pyotr Borisovich Kozlovski, caricature, ? 1813

Alexander Turgenev

It will be recalled that the social and cultural reforms introduced by the Russian rulers of the late eighteenth century, particularly Catherine II, had led to the emergence into prominence, during the first years of the new century, of a whole galaxy of talented men—writers, poets, publicists, educators, administrators, and diplomats—for the most part sons of the nobility or the land-owning gentry. A number of these men had collaborated hopefully and enthusiastically with the regime of Alexander I in its earlier liberal stages; but the greater conservatism of that Tsar in his final years tended to alienate them from the regime and to encourage the sort of conspiratorial and oppositional activity that found its culmination in the Decembrist insurrection of 1825. Some of these men were involved, of course, in the insurrection, and subsequently perished on the gallows or were sent to Siberia. Others, however, though sympathizing with the Decembrists, survived and continued, like the poet Pushkin, to circulate in Russian society and to pursue—with growing difficulty as the new reign of Nicholas I ran its course—their literary or public careers.

Of these last, many were from the start—from the time, that is, of the suppression of the Decembrist insurrection—deeply embittered men. Their self-confidence had been partly shaken, their youthful enthusiasms blasted by the tragic outcome of this episode. They were resentful towards the regime for what it had done, sympathetic to the victims of the repressive action, and often assailed by feelings of guilt over the fact of their own survival.

Now, on top of all of this, had come the Polish uprising of 1830-31, and its similar suppression. The effect on these people was much like what one suspects to have been the similar effect of the recent invasion of Czechoslovakia on members of the Soviet literary intelligentsia. Still smarting from the trauma of the Decembrist insurrection, it was impossible for them not to feel sympathy for the Poles. Yet they were stung in their national sensibilities and thrown onto the defensive by the torrents of criticism, much of it ill-informed and some of it malicious in intent, which the episode unleashed in western circles. Thus political idealism often was obliged to do battle with Russian patriotism within one and the same breast. These people could understand western sympathy for the Poles, but they could not endure the anti-Russianism that usually went with it. The conflict was well-expressed by Pushkin himself: "I despise my country from head to toe, but I am angry when a foreigner shares my feeling."

The conflicts of feeling and conscience unleashed by the Polish uprising and its consequences are perhaps best reflected in the literary works and personal relations of the two great poets: Pushkin and Mickiewicz. The latter had been living prior to the uprising in Petersburg, where he had been greatly respected and even lionized. He had entertained intimate and affectionate relations with a number of the great Russian writers of his day, including Pushkin, and had been accustomed to regarding himself as a member of the Russian literary world. Now, after the Polish uprising, he had joined the Polish exiles in Paris, and had written and published there the anti-Russian poem mentioned in Chapter II. That he had his Russian friends very much in mind when he wrote it, and that it was meant specifically for their eyes, was shown by the fact that he dedicated it to them; and the temper in which he wrote it was made evident in the biting words of the dedication—notably these:

> Now to the world I pour this poisoned chalice
> A bitter tale sucked forth from burning veins;
> My country's blood and tears compound its malice;
> Let it corrode—not you, friends, but your chains.[7]

Nothing could have struck more excruciatingly into the torn feelings of the Russian literati than such words, particularly coming as they did from the pen of a friend who was widely regarded as one of the greatest, if not the greatest, of the Slavic poets of his time. The force of their reaction found its expression in Pushkin's great poetic tale of *The Bronze Horseman,* a work in which he accepted Mickiewicz'

challenge, met it head-on by choosing the same symbol of
the equestrian statue of Peter the Great as the title and
positive focus of his poem, and then proceeded to intro-
duce the work by his magnificent opening paean to the
city of Petersburg—a paean that endorsed not just the
beauty of the city but the richness and color of its life.

When Custine undertook his journey to Russia, Pushkin
had been dead three years; but the anguish of this great
controversy still racked the literary and intellectual worlds
of Russia, Poland, and—to the extent people were interested in Russia at all—France. It was a controversy between, on the one hand, a negative, despairing view of
Russia—a view that saw as a failure the entire effort of
the eighteenth-century Russian rulers to bring that country
into Europe and into the modern age, and, on the other
hand, a positive, hopeful one—a view held almost exclusively by Russians themselves, and one based less on reason,
less on any observable or demonstrable fact, than on a realization of the heroic dimensions of the tragedy of Russian
life, a sense of being part of it, and a despairing faith that
somehow or other so much suffering could not be wholly
in vain—that someday something positive, something com-
mensurate with the enormity of the tragedy, must come out
of it.*

It must be emphasized that this was not always a conflict that divided individuals; it was often a conflict within
the individual Russian breast. And one has the impression
that among those members of the great literary and admin-
istrative intelligentsia of the period of Alexander I who
had remained alive and in Russia down to the end of the
1830's—people now no longer young and increasingly worn
down with frustration and disappointment—sensitivity to
western criticism, and with it a tendency to defend the
regime against criticism by foreigners, tended to increase,

---

* One is moved to recall, here, Tyutchev's famous lines:
   Russia is not to be grasped with the mind,
   There is no stick by which she can be measured.
   She has her own peculiar character.
   In Russia—one can only believe.

rather than to wane, with the years. They had now to defend themselves, in their own consciences, not only for the
fact that they had survived after 1825, whereas others had
suffered or perished, but also that they had remained in
Russia and made their peace with the regime, whereas
others, like Herzen or Mickiewicz, had emigrated. The resulting inner conflict left them touchy and defensive in
their relations with outsiders. It was men of this sort to
whom Custine was recommended; and we must assume
that Vyazemski and Chaadayev were not the only ones he
met in whom such feelings and reactions could be encountered.

If the men who were connected with Custine's journey
be examined in their relationship to this painful dichotomy
of opinion just described, it will be seen that they covered
the entire spectrum of reaction. Of the views of Bulgakov
or of Prince Odoyevski I have no adequate evidence. Vyazemski, I believe, was strongly on Pushkin's side. Chaadayev and Alexander Turgenev were torn between the two
points of view. Kozlovski, for whose outlooks Custine was
peculiarly receptive and who probably had the greatest influence on him, was definitely on the side of Mickiewicz.
This was the diversity of opinion to which Custine, strongly
under Polish-Catholic influence from the outset, was exposed during the course of his journey—at least insofar
as his letter from Turgenev and his encounters with Kozlovski were concerned.

IV. *CUSTINE IN RUSSIA*

ASIDE from long romantic descriptions of Petersburg and
Moscow, Custine's account of his actual travel in Russia
is remarkably thin. Of his experiences outside the two
capitals, in particular, very little is told. Even the record
of his experiences in the two great cities is obviously intentionally veiled and generally unsatisfactory. But a glance at
the high spots of his experience, as they emerge from his
account, will be helpful to an understanding of his book.

The *Nicholas I* anchored off Kronstadt, in the early summer
dawn of the far north, on July 10, 1839. It was at once
boarded by an army of customs and police officials—and
there ensued, throughout the hours of the morning, an inter-
minable ordeal of inspection in the grand salon of the
cabins. (This caused Custine to observe blandly, as his
first impression of Russia, that in the administration of that
country a concern for the *minutiae* did not exclude disorder.) The passengers were then placed on another vessel, of shallower draft, and taken up the ship canal to St.
Petersburg itself. (Custine noted at this point that the
cordiality, and the interest in him, previously manifested
by certain of the Russian passengers, fell off markedly as
they felt themselves back in the political atmosphere of
their native land.)

Once the vessel had docked at Petersburg, Custine's Russian friends were released, but he himself was held for a
further questioning—an ordeal in which most of the ques-

tions already asked him on the ship were now repeated.*
(In the administration of Russia, he observed at this point,
it was clear that one formality, successfully accomplished,
by no means excluded another.)

Custine remained in Petersburg, on that first occasion,
a little more than three weeks—until August 2. On July 14
he attended (it was his first appearance in court society)
the wedding, in the private chapel of the Winter Palace,
of the Emperor's daughter, Princess Olga (known as the
Grand Duchess Marie) to the French prince Maximilian
Joseph de Beauharnais, grandson of the Empress Josephine.
That same night, Custine, although not yet formally presented at court, was permitted, on intercession by the French

* Here is Custine's account of his interrogation by the crew of
officials at the pier in Petersburg:
What are you going to do in Russia?
    See the country.
That is no proper purpose for travel.
    I have no other.
Whom do you expect to see at Petersburg?
    All those who will permit me to make their acquaintance.
How long do you expect to stay in Russia?
    I don't know.
Tell me approximately.
    Some months.
Do you have a public diplomatic mission?
    No.
A secret one?
    No.
Some scientific purpose?
    No.
Have you been sent by your government to observe the social and
political situation in this country?
    No.
By some commercial enterprise, perhaps?
    No.
You are travelling independently and by pure curiosity?
    Yes.
Why did you choose Russia to come to?
    I don't know . . . etc., etc.
Do you have letters of recommendation to certain people in
this country?
    (I had been warned that it would be inconvenient to respond
    too frankly to this question, so I spoke only of the one I had
    from my banker.)

Ambassador, to attend the wedding ball, where he met the Emperor and Empress and spoke with both.

This day cannot have been an easy one for Custine. Except for the French Ambassador he knew almost no one at court. Attired in as much of a court costume as he could assemble from his travelling wardrobe, he was obliged to make his way to the Winter Palace alone, in a hired carriage. Descending from the carriage at the foot of the steps leading up to the palace, and before the eyes of the great crowd of onlookers held at a distance by the police, he caught the buckle of his slipper on some protuberance in the carriage door, and it tore off, leaving the slipper dangling on his foot. The footman at once slammed the door of the carriage behind him; and the unfeeling coachman drove smartly off, leaving him with one good shoe and one dragging one. He endured a moment of panic and despair. He could not run after the carriage, nor could he communicate effectively with the lackey who had slammed the door. There was nothing for it but to head up the staircase, for his first encounter with the Russian court, with one dragging shoe. But at this moment, the wisdom engendered by a long life of social rejection broke through to fortify him for the ordeal, and he comforted himself with the penetrating reflection (it is one of those inimitable touches that make his books worth reading) that nothing of this nature that happens to a person is ever really as important to other people as it is to him.

In the Bolshoi Theatre's staging of Pushkin's *Eugene Onegin*, there is a magnificent ballroom scene, depicting one of the great Petersburg routs of Custine's period, in which all of the male members of the huge company on stage are in resplendent court uniform except the hero himself, Onegin, who, just back in Russia after years abroad, estranged from the society of St. Petersburg and knowing no one but the host, wanders forlornly around, the sole person dressed in black, ignored and abandoned by all the others. Thus poor Custine, one imagines, must have felt himself at the wedding ball. He was wearing, he recounts,

an Arabian talisman given to his mother, through the bars
of her prison cell, by the grandfather of the present bride-
groom, as he passed down the prison corridor on the way
to his own execution in the Terror. Custine was too proud,
however, to invite attention to this. It was a warm night,
heavy with the occasional oppressive heat of the far-north-
ern summer and the emanations of the sweltering crowd;
and he recounts that when the Empress, to his intense
gratification, sought him out and spoke to him, he had
sought refuge in an empty alcove by an open window,
where he could breathe the fresh night air and look out
on the beauty of the city in the fabulous "white night" of
early summer. Thus one is moved to picture him, as he entered upon his visit to Russia: a vain, defensive, and sensitive man, bearing the scars of a long ordeal of disgrace and
opprobrium, quick to sense arrogance or ridicule with relation to himself, but intensely grateful for any really civilized and tactful attention.

Custine attended two other balls given in connection
with the Beauharnais wedding: one by the Emperor's sister,
the Grand Duchess Hélène, at her residence in the Palais
Michel, where he again met the Emperor and Empress, the
other—a *fête champêtre* at the suburban villa of the Duchess of Oldenburg. Then, from the 23rd to the 27th of July,
he was a guest of the Imperial couple at the great fete
given annually at the suburban palace of Peterhof, where
the Tsar and his wife received as guests, and entertained,
for some three days, people of all ranks of Russian society,
from the nobility down to the peasantry. Custine, being a
latecomer and all the regular guest suites being already
occupied, found himself installed, rather ridiculously, in
one of the actors' dressing rooms of the summer theatre.
This ignominy was outweighed, however, by the fact that
he was, through the intercession of Gurowski's half-sister,
permitted to pay a visit of inspection to the private "cot-
tage" of the Imperial couple. Here he encountered, by one
of those contrived accidents sometimes arranged for the

purpose of circumventing the protocol of royal courts, the Empress herself, and was able to put young Gurowski's case to her. She heard him out, but then fell silent. He pocketed the reverse, comforting himself with the fancy that he could imagine the doubts present in her mind at that moment—the question as to what the future of such a young Pole would be at the Russian court in the event the request were granted: the lack of any normal social base, the jealousy and resentment of the older Russian courtiers, the experience of growing old in a false position.

At the time of the Peterhof festival, Custine asked permission, through the Minister of War, to visit the fortress of Schlüsselburg, situated on an island at the head of the Neva River, where that great stream flows out of Lake Ladoga. The request, at once passed on to the Emperor, surely occasioned some surprise, for this sinister bastion was the favored place of detention for particularly important and dangerous prisoners of state. It was here that the miserable imperial pretender of the mid-eighteenth century, Ivan VI, had been literally buried alive for twenty-three years, in deepest isolation and silence, until his murder by his guards in 1764. Custine had a very definite weakness for the morbid; and it was unquestionably the tales of the miserable fate of Ivan VI that had aroused his desire to see this place.

A few days later, on the eve of his intended departure from Petersburg, the request was granted—but only in the form of a permission to visit *the locks* at Schlüsselburg. He made the excursion, nevertheless. It was perhaps his most horrible day in Russia. His nerves were on edge, his apprehensions aroused. An officer, assigned to escort him, seemed to him to be his jailer rather than his host. He tortured himself on the outward journey with the thought: "What if this escort and this carriage were to keep right on going and eventually deliver me to some far-Siberian confinement? It could easily be said in Petersburg that I had accidentally fallen into the river and drowned. Who would know?"

He was to be much ridiculed in later years for the confession of these fears in his book; and they must indeed appear ridiculous to anyone who has never had the experience of being in a country where secrecy is ubiquitous, and power arbitrary and unlimited. Despite his timidity, Custine showed remarkable persistence in his purpose. He succeeded, almost miraculously, in eventually talking his way into the fortress itself, to the acute embarrassment of all concerned. But the whole experience was a dreadful one. Its sinister quality would long haunt his imagination and affect his view of Russia.

On one occasion, while in Petersburg, Custine paid a visit to an unidentified "prince ***," a "*grand seigneur*," who, one would think, could only have been, once again, Kozlovski. He found him living alone, in the empty, barnlike palace of his absent sister, "*ruiné, infirme, malade, hydropique,*" unable to rise from the wooden bench on which, in default of a bed, he was installed.

But what of Vyazemski and Odoyevski, to whom Custine had been recommended? There is no record of his having seen either. One suspects that he must have seen Vyazemski, or tried to see him, and have been in some way rebuffed; for while at no other point does he mention by name any of those listed in Turgenev's letter, he goes out of his way, at one point in the book, to mention a monograph Vyazemski had written on the burning of the Winter Palace and to refer to him, offensively and certainly unjustly, as a "courtier." That Vyazemski did not fail to notice this slight, and to take it in part, is shown by his subsequent correspondence with Turgenev as well as by a certain passage in his comments on Custine's book, written nearly five years later. But beyond that, we have this curious passage, embodied in those same comments:

As for the reception accorded to M. de Custine by Russian society, I have no knowledge of it, and I am not the only one to have no knowledge of it. One thing is certain: and this is that the noble marquis was never encountered in any of the salons of the capital ordinarily frequented by travellers of distinction.[1]

What is one to make of this? Odoyevski's salon answered precisely to this description. And Vyazemski's own home? Was Custine not received there, despite Turgenev's recommendation? The mystery remains. Only one thing is clear. Custine and Vyazemski emerged from the episode of Custine's visit to Russia with a strong dislike for each other.

On August 2, as mentioned above, Custine set forth for Moscow, travelling in his own English carriage. He was accompanied by Antonio and a Russian *feldjaeger* assigned to him by the government—a man whom he soon came to detest and who, to all appearances, heartily reciprocated the sentiment. As motive power he was obliged, like all other travellers of means and position, to use the relays of post-horses by which one was moved from one to the other of the postal stations, situated at intervals of about eight miles. He was warned that his carriage, however fine the English workmanship, would be too delicate for the Russian roads, and this proved to be true. There were breakdowns and delays. Within five days, however, averaging something over seventy-five miles a day, he had arrived in Moscow and installed himself in the inn kept there by the English Madame Howard. It had, as he understood it, the reputation of being the only clean hostelry in Russia.

Custine spent nine days in Moscow on that occasion. The first three were passed in a seclusion forced upon him by an eye infection contracted from the dust of the Russian highways. During the remaining six days he did intensive sight-seeing and was entertained on several occasions. He liked Moscow better than Petersburg. The air seemed freer, the talk less constrained. He was taken out to a luncheon party in the garden of a rather luxurious dacha, where he even, for once, admired the company and enjoyed their conversation. Like everyone else, he was impressed by the barbaric splendor and confusion of Moscow architecture.

He lost himself in speculations about how vast and impressive would be Russian power if the seat of it were ever to be moved from Petersburg to Moscow: only then, he thought, would Russia's destiny be finally achieved.

It is impossible to tell how much Custine saw, in Moscow, of the persons mentioned in Turgenev's letter. His host at the garden luncheon party was presumably either Sverbeyev or Bulgakov. As for Chaadayev, there is real mystery. Custine describes at one point in his book, as though from hearsay, a man who could be none other than Chaadayev, and goes out of his way to say that he did not see him personally. Sverbeyev, on the other hand, states in his memoirs that he did; and Sverbeyev would have known. Record has survived of a cryptic note from Chaadayev to his cousin, Princess E. D. Shcherbatova (sister-in-law, evidently, of Sverbeyeva), in which he asks her to make known, or to cause to be made known, to Custine *"ce qu'il faut qu'il sache."** Thus there *was* communication of some sort.

There is, finally, Custine's long account of a conversation he had, in the garden of the famous English Club in Moscow, with a Russian gentleman whose name he does not reveal. The tenor of this account has aroused considerable speculation as to the identity of the interlocutor. Conceivably, it might have been Turgenev or Kozlovski or Chaadayev. All were, or could have been, in Moscow at that time. Although the views quoted and other indications do not seem wholly to fit Chaadayev, they fit him far better than they do either of the other two; and there can be little doubt, I think, that it was he with whom Custine conversed.†

* Custine's obvious reference to Chaadayev will be found in the *Résumé du Voyage, La Russie,* IV, 378-381. The passage in Sverbeyev's memoirs is cited in Cadot, *op.cit.,* p. 215. The note from Chaadayev to Shcherbatova may be found in M. Gershenzon, *P. Ya. Chaadayev, Socheneniya i pis'ma,* Moscow, 1913, I, 239.

† The evidence is complex. The flattering terms in which Custine refers to his interlocutor resemble those used in the obvious reference to Chaadayev in the *Résumé du Voyage.* They are ones that would, as we shall see shortly, scarcely have been used with relation to Turgenev. Furthermore, the man he talked with was, Custine says,

Whether there was only one such conversation or whether several took place, we do not know. It would even be dangerous to rely on Custine's account of what passed in the discussion between the two men. But that Chaadayev's ideas, what between the *Philosophic Letter* and these personal exchanges, made a deep impression on Custine, and found reflection in some degree in his view of Russia, there can be no doubt.

Custine departed for Yaroslavl and Nizhni Novgorod on August 16. He left his English carriage behind in Moscow and rented, this time, a Russian one which his friends assured him would be stronger. This view, as it happened, proved to be over-optimistic. The journey continued to be plagued by the tedium of repeated breakdowns and repairs.

The first stop was at the present Zagorsk* where, like many a foreign visitor of a later day, Custine proposed to visit the famous Troitse-Sergievskaya monastery. Here, at Zagorsk, he was overtaken by a gentleman who, he explains, had left Moscow several hours after him. From the description, this could hardly have been any other than Alexander Turgenev. He is known to have proceeded to Russia, that summer, shortly after Custine but by a different route. Whether they had seen each other in the meantime is not established; but since they had both been in Moscow as recently as the previous day, they may be presumed to have done so.

During his change of horse-relays, Turgenev asked to see Custine. There then ensued, presumably at the postal station, a most curious verbal exchange, the account of which

---

the man who introduced him at the English Club. Chaadayev was a member of the Club, and frequented it. Exhibiting pro-Catholic sympathies, Custine's interlocutor nevertheless showed himself a non-Catholic by saying that he envied Custine his faith. This excludes Kozlovski, who was understood by Custine to be a practicing Catholic.

* The place was at that time not called by that name, but more generally known by the name of the monastery. For purposes of convenience, I shall use here the name "Zagorsk" to indicate the place in question.

by Custine only deepens the mystery of the relations between the two men. Custine, evidently, had already heard
rumors of peasant disorders in the region of Simbirsk. This,
as it happened, was the region in which Turgenev had his
estates. It was presumably to this destination that he was
hurrying. Custine evidently asked Turgenev about this, and
Turgenev, by Custine's account, now confirmed to him that
eighty villages had indeed been burned, in the *gouvernement* of Simbirsk, by revolting peasants. He went on to say,
however, that Russians tended to attribute this unrest to
intrigues on the part of the Poles. The latter, he intimated,
did such things with provocative intent, precisely to arouse
further Russian ire and to dissuade the Emperor from show-
ing any greater clemency towards Poland, lest the Polish
peasantry be moved to take a kinder view of the Russians.

This curious suggestion evoked a sultry and bitter reply
from Custine. "I prefer to believe," he said, "that the Russians hurl accusations at their victims in order to justfy
their own rancor, and that they search, in everything unfortunate that happens to them, for some pretext to make
heavier the yoke they impose on their adversaries, whose
ancient glory they view as an unpardonable crime."

"You take a poor view of our policies," replied Turgenev,
"because you don't know either the Russians or the Poles."

"That," rejoined Custine, "is the usual refrain of your
compatriots when anyone tells them any unpleasant truth."
And then, moving over to what was clearly a personal
note, he proceeded to point out that the Poles were easy
to know, because they were always talking; he, however,
had more confidence in garrulous people of this sort, who
said everything, than he had in "taciturn men who say only
those things that no one would want to know."

Just who it was, among the Russians, against whom this
sally was directed, is not clear. Turgenev was surely not a
taciturn man. But he took it personally. *"Il faut pourtant,"*
he said, *"que vous ayez bien de la confiance en moi."*

"In you personally—yes," replied Custine, "but when I

remember that you are a Russian it makes no difference that I have known you for ten years; I still reproach myself for my imprudence—that is to say, for my frankness."

"I foresee," observed Turgenev bitterly, "that you are going to deal harshly with us when you get back home."

"If I write anything, perhaps," returned Custine, "but, as you say, I don't know the Russians, and I shall take care never to speak lightly of that impenetrable nation."

"That is the best thing you could do."

"À *la bonne heure*," said Custine, in terminating the conversation, "but don't forget that the most reserved men, known once to have dissimulated, are viewed thenceforth as having been demasked."

With this, Custine says, "my old friend climbed into his carriage and departed at a gallop; as for me, I returned to my chambers to write down for you this dialogue."[2]

What, once again, is one to make of this curious encounter? The exchange has by no means the ring of a conversation between two men who knew each other only casually and just happened to run into each other in a small provincial town in Russia. Surely, something further had intervened. What was Turgenev doing, anyway, in Zagorsk? It was not on the direct route to Simbirsk. And why was he in such a hurry? Why, in fact, since he and Custine were old acquaintances, since it was he who had given Custine his recommendations in Russia, and since they were evidently leaving Moscow within a few hours of each other and travelling by the same route, did he not travel in Custine's company? There could of course have been wholly unrelated reasons for all these things. But were there?

Turgenev, like Custine, was obviously en route to Yaroslavl. He presumably arrived there very shortly before Custine did. Custine evidently expected to see him there; otherwise, why the "*à la bonne heure?*" But then one encounters, in Custine's account of his reception by the governor at Yaroslavl, the following curious passage:

No one expected me at Yaroslavl. I decided to take that route only on the eve of the day of my departure from Moscow. And despite the formality of Russian *amour-propre*, I was not a sufficiently important man in the eyes of the person from whom I requested, at the last moment, certain letters of introduction, to suppose that he would have me preceded by a courier.[3]

Was this not perhaps an elaborate and polite way of voicing a strong suspicion? Let us recall the circumstances. On August 15, on the eve of his departure from Moscow, Custine suddenly decided to travel to Nizhni Novgorod by way of Zagorsk and Yaroslavl instead of by the usual route via Vladimir. Before taking his departure, he hastily solicited and procured from someone, almost certainly Turgenev's intimate friend Bulgakov, in any case someone who would have had the authority to have him preceded by a courier, letters of introduction to the governor and others in Yaroslavl. He then left Moscow. Only a few hours later Turgenev left, behind him, overtook him at Zagorsk, inquired after him there, and hastened on ahead. Was Custine's professed assurance that he supposed he was not important enough to be preceded by a courier not an ironic hint at what he now supposed to have been the case?

Custine was charmed by the reception he received at the hands of the governor in Yaroslavl, General K. M. Poltoratski, and by the sophisticated Parisian conversation of the latter's wife and the old French governess who lived at their home. When first observing the elegance of the equipage which the governor sent to bring him to the residence, he had been afraid, he confessed, that he was going to encounter only more of those "*Européens voyageurs, les courtisans de l'Empereur Alexandre—les grands seigneurs cosmopolites*" whom he had encountered in Petersburg and had come so cordially to dislike.[*] He was therefore not

---

[*] Surely, one must suppose, he had Vyazemski in mind when writing this phrase—perhaps also Odoyevski and Turgenev.

only pleasantly surprised but emotionally overwhelmed to find himself in a house where speech and manners and subjects of conversation all put him back into the atmosphere of his youth. His stay in Yaroslavl was, however, of brief duration. On the 21st he was off again to Nizhni Novgorod.

Although the governor at Nizhni, Prince M. P. Buturlin, was no less hospitable to him than his colleague in Yaroslavl, Custine's stay there was less agreeable. He was poorly housed. He disliked the chance assembly of itinerant foreigners—French, British, even Americans—in whose company he was entertained by the governor. He fell ill with a chill and was obliged to take to his bed. A Russian physician, summoned to his bedside, advised him only to get out of Nizhni Novgorod, however ill he might be, without delay. Custine took the advice, was at once restored, and arrived safely at Moscow on September 4.

His brief stay of four days at Moscow on this occasion was only a transit stop. On the 8th he was off again for Petersburg, travelling once more in his own carriage—but only after involving himself actively and indignantly, against the advice of the French consul and of a high Russian official (probably Bulgakov), in the affair of a young Frenchman who had been arrested and was, for reasons unstated, being held incommunicado by the Russian authorities.

Arriving back in Petersburg approximately September 8, Custine spent nearly another fortnight in that city before setting forth, by the land route this time, on the return to Western Europe. This second visit to Petersburg is almost a blank spot in the narrative. He tells us almost nothing about it, other than that he did a bit of sight-seeing. The court was no longer in town. The summer doldrums were at their height. He was taken on one occasion by a princely acquaintance to see the "arsenal" (evidently an artillery plant) at Kolpino, which bored him mightily. He also visited the museum of art, and was unimpressed. But this, which is about all that emerges from the account given in the book, could scarcely have been all there was. One suspects that if one knew what were his experiences, and with whom he was in contact, during this final fortnight, one would be able to solve a number of the mysteries of his journey.

Custine had thought originally to return to Eastern Europe via Poland, visiting Vilna and Warsaw. He changed this plan, however, and chose in preference the route through East Prussia. Why? He offered an explanation. The Poles, he intimates, had their faults. People did not suffer as the Poles had suffered without having some degree of complicity in their own misfortunes. If he were to view their sufferings at first hand he would be moved, he feared, to reflections of which he would afterwards repent. To speak the truth to oppressors was a duty which, sustained as one was by the sense of courage and generosity derived from assailing such an opponent, one took upon one's self with pleasure. But to vex the victim, to burden the oppressed, if only by the blows of truth: this was something to which no writer could stoop who did not despise his own pen.

What had happened? Why these sudden reservations about the Poles? Had Custine been talking further, during these final two weeks, with Kozlovski? The latter, while a friend of the Poles, was too wise and experienced a man not to be aware of their weaknesses. Perhaps Kozlovski feared embarrassment to himself, and to Paskevich, from a visit by Custine to Poland. He might well have had reason to.

On September 26, Custine crossed the border at Tilsit. His joy and relief were enormous. A bird escaped from the cage could not, he said, have been happier. He had emerged "from the empire of uniformity, of formalities, of difficulties." One was, to be sure, only in Prussia; and Prussia, admittedly, did not pass exactly for the land of great freedom. But what a change! The houses, one saw at a glance, had been soundly and independently built—not erected by slaves at the orders of an inflexible master. The countryside was cheerful and well-cultivated. And people spoke freely. In passing through the streets of Tilsit and Königsberg, he felt himself, by comparison with Russia, to be "attending the Carnival of Venice." At last he could breathe.

Thus—the record of Custine's journey. Most of it, in the personal sense, remains shrouded in obscurity. The bits that show above the surface are fragmentary, unsatisfactory, suggestive, and tantalizing.

The correspondence of Turgenev and Vyazemski and Bulgakov does not suggest that Custine played any very important part in their lives; and the same, no doubt, would surely have been true of Kozlovski. For them, Custine was an odd and slightly disreputable French character, whom it was uncomfortable to have around. But what part did they play in *his* life? And were there others involved who helped to shape his views, his aversions, his resentments?

The evidence yields no answer. This visit to Russia was, obviously, an unhappy experience, endured by a twisted, over-sensitive man, to whose aesthetic and physical sensibilities the Russia of that day was generally offensive, and to whose delicate psychic constitution, already chafed and tender from personal misfortune of long standing, it was nothing other than sinister and abhorrent.

V. THE BOOK

CUSTINE, on his return from Russia, seemed in no hurry to write his book. The autumn of 1839 was passed with a well-deserved rest at a German spa. Then there was the season in Paris—no time to write books.

In the summer of the following year, 1840, he brought Gurowski to Germany and presented him to the Russian Empress, who was taking the cure at one of the German watering-places. He still evidently had hopes at that time that the young man might be readmitted. Had this been the case, the book, one must suppose, might never have been written, or it might at least have been a very different book; for Gurowski, had he been in Russia at the time of the appearance of *La Russie en 1839* could not have failed to suffer, as indeed his half-sister did, from the displeasure the work evoked in high Russian circles.

But there was no relenting in the Emperor's firm determination not to let people of Gurowski's ilk return to the Empire. And if Custine was willing to wait, Gurowski himself was not. In the months following his presentation to the Empress, he launched himself upon a series of scandals and adventures that ended with his elopement with the Spanish *infanta* and their removal to Brussels. Custine, be it said to his credit, did not lose interest in the young man as a consequence of this abandonment of the celibate state: he even visited the young couple at Brussels and commiserated with them in their impoverished and exiled plight. But he must have realized at this point that there could now be no question of Gurowski's return to Russia; and this barrier to the writing of the book, if indeed it was a barrier, was now removed.

In the autumn of 1841, therefore, Custine, seeking relief in Switzerland and Italy from the fatigues of Paris social life, composed himself once more to the task of authorship, and within the space of approximately one year, the 1800-page work was substantially completed.

The book took the form of thirty-one long letters to an anonymous French friend, written ostensibly during and just after the journey of the summer of 1839. The device was not wholly artificial. Custine did apparently contrive to write and smuggle out one or more letters during the period of his stay in Russia. These he presumably recovered and drew upon in the writing of the book. But by far the greater part of the material was evidently composed for the first time in 1841-42; and in general the casting of this material in the form of letters from various points visited during his journey was an artificiality (not uncommon in the literature of the day) which cannot have been intended to deceive anyone.

The first three of the letters had very little to do with Russia and could, for the most part, just as well have been omitted from the account.* Another letter, in the body of the work, was devoted to the highly-embroidered and romanticized recounting of a tale from Russian peasant life which someone had told him. For the rest, however, the letters purported to give the impressions of the journey.

Many of these impressions were aesthetic: long descriptions of landscape and architecture in the romantic style of the period. There are also numerous anecdotes and legends, almost exclusively second-hand, which Custine saw fit to include. For all of these he has been severely,

* While passing through Berlin, Custine was given access, by the French envoy there, to materials about his grandfather's activity as commander of the armies on the Rhine. He took this as the point of departure for an account of his parents' misfortunes which pre-empted most of these first three letters.

and often justly, taken to task by his many critics. It is not on these passages, however, that the enduring value of the book has rested. It is rather the many political reactions, often expressed in biting aphorisms and witticisms appealing to some readers, infuriating to others, but always striking and provocative, that have given to the work its extraordinary longevity of relevance. These reactions constitute, in their entirety, one view of the Russian government and society of that day. It is a view not easy for any outsider to recapitulate, because so much of its color lay in the language in which it was stated. The following observations and citations, however, may give some idea of its salient features—particularly those that have attracted the attention of the readers of our own time.

It will be easier to understand Custine's reactions if one has in mind the views on political institutions with which he entered upon his journey. They were, by his own account, not dissimilar to those with which Tocqueville had embarked on the journey to America. Custine, like Tocqueville, was preoccupied with the decline in the influence of the French aristocracy which had set in with the Revolution and had continued even after the Restoration. He viewed with fear and distrust the egalitarian tendencies that seemed to be pervading and overwhelming French society in the age of Louis Philippe. He was of course on principle a monarchist, because it was impossible for him to conceive of an aristocracy without a monarchy. But he was by no means a protagonist of personal absolutism. "Being an aristocrat by character as well as conviction," he wrote,

> I consider that only an aristocracy can resist the seductions as well as the abuses of absolute power. Without an aristocracy there would be nothing but tyranny in monarchies as well as in democracies. The spectacle of despotism revolts me in spite of myself and violates all the ideas of liberty that flow from my intimate feelings and my political beliefs. Despotism can be born

of unlimited egalitarianism just as well as it can be born of autocracy. The power of a single man and the power of all men together conduce to the same end. . . .[1]

Holding these views, Custine was of course suspicious of the power of electoral majorities. To place nations at the mercy of such majorities was to subject them, he said, to mediocrity. Democratic government was the government of words, not acts. The statesmanship of the multitude was always "timid, avaricious, and mean."[2] And all this being so, he had no kindly feelings, in principle, towards the concept of a constitutional monarchy. He even claimed, in the *avant-propos* to the second authorized edition of his work, that he went to Russia "to seek arguments against representative government."[3]

On the other hand, he recognized that such views were now under heavy challenge and attack in Western Europe; and one suspects that he had himself been somewhat shaken in his attachment to them, probably by the reading of Tocqueville's first volume of *De la Démocratie en Amérique* —shaken not in the sense that he had been weaned away from them or convinced of their opposite, but rather in the sense that he found himself devoid of arguments with which to refute the conclusions Tocqueville had drawn from his American journey. Custine's conviction of the essentiality of aristocracy, as an institution, and his abhorrence of egalitarianism, remained firm, throughout. But on the question whether the institution of monarchy should or should not be accompanied by anything in the nature of a parliamentary body, and whether such an arrangement should have its foundation in constitutional provisions limiting the power of the throne: on these questions his feelings, on available evidence, were muddled and uncertain at the time when he entered upon his journey.

This ambivalence was well-reflected in the account he gives of a talk he had with the Emperor, Nicholas I, soon after arrival in Russia. As to the literal accuracy of this account, one must reserve judgment. The claim on the part of historical personages to recall at a later date the exact words used by themselves and other parties in long conversations is bound to inspire a certain uneasiness in the historian. But the passage, whether literally accurate or not, may safely be taken as reflecting some of Custine's own hesitations on the subject in question.

The Emperor, according to this account, expressed to Custine his strong aversion to the concept of a constitutional monarchy. He did not deny that his own government was a personal despotism. Despotism, he said, was the very essence of his government. But, he said, it was a form of government that accorded with the temper of the nation. "I can conceive," he went on,

> of a republic. It is a proper and sincere form of government—or at least it can be. I can also conceive of an absolute monarchy since I am, after all, at the head of such an arrangement. What I cannot conceive of is a constitutional monarchy. It is a government of the lie, of fraud, of corruption; and I would rather retreat as far as China, if need be, than ever adopt it.

To this, Custine quotes himself as replying (somewhat grandiloquently):

> Sire, I have always regarded representative government as a compromise inevitable in certain societies and at certain times; but like all compromises, it solves no problem—it only postpones the difficulty. . . . It is a truce of sorts, concluded between democracy and monarchy under the auspices of two very mean tyrants: fear and self-interest; and it is sustained and prolonged by the pride of spirit that satisfies itself with loquaciousness, and by the popular vanity that accepts its rewards in words.

The Emperor responded to this pronouncement, the account continues, by warmly shaking Custine's hand and saying: "Monsieur, you speak the truth"; after which he went on to refer (obviously, with the recent Polish uprising

of 1830-31 in mind) to the difficulties he himself had experienced in his effort to fill the role of a constitutional
monarch in Poland.[4]

How much of what Custine quotes himself as saying on
this occasion was sincere, and how much was the product
of a natural anxiety to be tactful and courteous in the discussion of this delicate subject with an absolute monarch,
is not easy to determine; but his description of representative government as a "compromise inevitable in certain
societies and at certain times"—a view which we may take
as almost certainly influenced by Tocqueville—is clearly
indicative of the torn and contradictory feelings with which,
during the period in question, he reflected on the proper
role of popular representation in the pattern of modern
government.

This is perhaps a good point at which to note that Custine's
attitude towards the person of the Emperor was also one
of the most painful, almost tortured, ambivalence. Few
critics have failed to spot as one of the great weaknesses
of this book the contradictory and, in its totality, uncon-
vincing manner in which Custine dealt with the Imperial
person. There are evidences, on the one hand, of a desire to
please and flatter the Emperor, and to commiserate with
him on the difficulty of the task of ruling so great an empire
with so unhappy a past.*

On the other hand, as Custine's indictment of the Russian
political system gathered power throughout the book, and
as the examples mounted of the unlimited personal power
of the supreme sovereign, it became impossible to main-
tain the pose of absolving the Tsar of all blame for existing
conditions. Custine finally faced up to this situation, towards
the end of his account, with characteristic pithiness and

* In a letter to Madame Récamier, commenting on the more favorable view of Russia entertained by the French ambassador in Petersburg, M. de Barante, Custine wrote: "After all, if one were to pass
one's life together with the imperial family, one *would* love Russia:
it represents without question all of the best that there is in this
country."[5]

incisiveness. "If the Emperor," he wrote, "has no more of mercy in his heart than he reveals in his policies, then I pity Russia; if, on the other hand, his true sentiments are really superior to his acts, then I pity the Emperor."[6]

That Custine was utterly fascinated by the Emperor—that he studied him with intense, almost passionate interest, that the person of the Emperor meant more to him than that of any other individual he encountered in Russia—is clear. In part this lay, no doubt, with the great fascination normally exerted over others by men who wield great power. There was also the matter of Gurowski and the importance of the Emperor's favor in connection with his possible return. But beyond this, one senses that Custine had, initially, a certain hope that he could ingratiate himself even beyond the normal possibilities of a foreign visitor and that he could win from the Emperor a form of personal interest and friendship that would give him real intimacy and influence at court. Had this hope been gratified, which it was not, his book would probably never have been written; for the hope was obliged to do battle in his mind, over the entire course of his journey, with the growing horror of his impressions of Russian conditions and the mounting impossibility of evading or concealing the fact of the Emperor's primary responsibility for them. Custine was confronted in the end with a choice: either to describe conditions and experiences that constituted, inescapably, an implicit reproach to the Emperor, or not to write any book at all. It is to the resulting conflict in his feelings that there must be attributed those contradictions and *non sequiturs* in the treatment of the Emperor to which so many foreign critics have drawn attention.

Quite aside from the person of the Emperor, Custine was not long in reacting negatively to the absolutism of the imperial position, as a political institution. He should not, perhaps, have been quite so unprepared for this. His companion on the ship, Prince Kozlovski, had warned him of it. *"Chez nous,"* the prince had said, "despotism is stronger than nature: the Emperor is not only the representative of God—he is the embodiment of the creative power itself."[7] Nevertheless, Custine was taken aback by what he encountered on arrival. He had not pictured it quite this way. "There does not exist today on the face of the earth," he was moved to exclaim, soon after his arrival, "a single other man who enjoys such power and uses it—not in Turkey, not even in China."[8] And what appalled him was not so much the absolute personal power over the *actions* of men: it was rather the power over their thoughts and words— in effect over their souls. He had the initial impression that everything he heard in Petersburg was only the reflection of some sort of party line, so to speak, put forward from above. "Among this people deprived of leisure and of will," he reflected, "one sees only bodies without souls, and one shudders upon reflecting that for so great a multitude of arms and legs there is only one head."[9] This led him to the realization that something more important than just political rights in the legal sense had been sacrificed to the Emperor's personal power: namely, individual dignity and independence of character. It was not that these things were wholly non-existent, not that no one enjoyed them or gave at least the appearance of enjoying them; it was rather that no one could depend upon them: they could not be taken for granted. "In Russia," he wrote, with an air of surprise and discovery, "tolerance has no guarantee, either in public opinion or in the constitution of the State; like everything else, it is a species of grace imposed by one man; and that one man can withdraw tomorrow what he has extended today."[10]

It was, however, as we have seen, not the institution of monarchy but rather that of aristocracy to which Custine looked to provide the keystone of any sound political structure; and it was here, accordingly, that he experienced his greatest disillusionment. Although himself an aristocrat, as he himself put it, "by character as well as conviction," and a firm supporter of the monarchical principle, Custine appears to have had a real distaste for court life and a certain contempt for the courtier, aristocratic or otherwise.* His concept of aristocracy was that of the independent *grand seigneur* of aristocratic lineage who had the dignity not only of his rank but also of his country estates or his fortune and whose status was in no way dependent on the royal or imperial favor. Possibly his distaste for the courtier was the product of his own unhappy experience when attached, in his youth, to the suite of Louis XVIII (then "Monsieur"). However this may be, he was particularly revolted by the atmosphere of the Russian court and the character of the nobility who composed it. He recognized this as being primarily only another mirror-image of the Emperor's absolute authority. Under the shadow of that authority all other distinctions of rank and caste seemed to lose meaning. Elsewhere, the superior distinction of birth was an independent possession, of which no nobleman could normally be deprived. Here, in Russia, it had no independent value. Like everything else, it was a product of the Emperor's favor. He could extend it; he could withdraw it. All these pompous courtiers, Custine suddenly realized, were no more than slaves themselves. They could be made or broken in a day. And the effect was to depress all of society beyond the imperial person itself into a virtual egalitarianism as sweeping and as odious in Custine's eyes as that which he understood to exist in the American democracy described by Tocqueville. When he attended the Peterhof fete, marked as it was by the theory that the Emperor and Empress were receiving at a single social occasion guests from all ranks of Russian society from top to bottom, it occurred to him that what was implicit in this imperial gesture of hospitality was not that the Emperor was saying to the laborer or to the merchant: "You are a man like myself," but rather that he was saying to the *grand*

---

* Note above, page 66, in this connection, Custine's contemptuous reference to "les courtisans de l'Empereur Alexandre," and also, page 60, his offensive reference to Vyazemski as a "courtier."

seigneur: "You are a slave, like them: and I, your god, soar equally above both your heads."[11]

But beyond this ignominy of position vis-à-vis the Emperor, there was much in the personal behavior of these Russian aristocrats and courtiers for which Custine could find only contempt. True, his observations were drawn largely from the people he saw at court, during the first days of his visit to the Russian capital. For reasons already noted, the doors of the more independent and distinguished noble houses in Petersburg were evidently closed to him— a circumstance that no doubt added to his bitterness. When he came away from the capital and travelled in other parts of the country, people were more hospitable, and he met some in whom he recognized a higher quality. But by and large, the opinion he formed of his own counterparts among the Russian nobility was unflattering in the extreme. He found them false, insincere, without independence of character or taste. He was constantly made aware of the savage intensity of their competition for the imperial favor. He observed in their behavior cruelty and officiousness towards underlings combined with the most extravagant obsequiousness towards people higher in position than themselves—a servility, as he described it, "gratuitous and involuntary, which does not exclude arrogance"[12]—a servility borne by people who were themselves only *"une espèce d'esclaves supérieurs."*[13] The actions of these people purported to be their own, but they were really those of an external will, and the pretense was too obvious to be accepted. They reminded him, he said, of "puppets whose strings were too thick."[14]

Even more odious, to Custine's taste, were the efforts of upper-class Russians to imitate the West. He could not endure the caricature of himself that seemed to him to emerge from their aping of Parisian customs and manners. It was all too obvious, too pathetic. The veneer of European civilization was too thin to be credible. The outlines of Asia shone through at every point. These Russian courtiers had taken on, he said, just enough of the gloss of European civilization to be "spoiled as savages," but not enough to become cultivated men. They were like (and I use his words) "trained bears who made you long for the wild ones."[15]

Custine gradually became aware that this intolerable gap between outer pretense and inner reality was only a single reflection of something broader and more serious still— something that came to constitute, one feels, the true focal point of his indictment of the regime of Nicholas I. This was the terrible, cynical, demeaning contempt for the truth that seemed to pervade Russian government and society. The behavior of the entire governing establishment appeared to be based on the cultivation of a series of massive fictions—fictions not just subconsciously and innocently appropriated into the minds of the bearers but deliberately conceived, perpetrated, and enforced. He found himself confronted at every turn with two images of Russian reality: the image of Russia as it really was, and the image of Russia as the authorities—and not, unfortunately, the authorities alone—wished it to appear. And he could never accustom himself to, or forgive, the cynicism with which everyone, from the Emperor on down, played at this game of make-believe and attempted to enthrone the false, artificial image at the expense of the real one.

Under the impact of this cultivated untruthfulness the whole façade of Russian social and official life began to appear to him as contrived, artificial, unreal. "I came here to see a country," he wrote,

> What I find is a theatre. . . . The names are the same as everywhere else. . . . In appearances everything happens as it does everywhere else. There is no difference except in the very foundation of things.[16]

He tended to attribute this passion for pretense to a consuming inferiority complex vis-à-vis the West, to an insatiable desire on the part of the Russians to appear to be what they were in reality incapable of being. And he had no sympathy or patience for these impulses. They disgusted him. "I don't reproach the Russians," he wrote,

> for being what they are; what I blame them for is their desire to appear to be what we are. . . . They are much less interested in being civilized than in making us believe them so. . . . They would be quite content to be in effect more awful and barbaric than they actually are, if only others could thereby be made to believe them better and more civilized. . . .[17]

In preference to this, he observed, even "a tyranny avowed would be a form of progress."[18]

Here again, he had been forewarned by Kozlovski. "Our government," the prince had said to him,

> lives by the lie, for the truth frightens the tyrant no less than the slave. . . . The people, and even the grandees, resigned spectators of this war against the truth, endure uncomplainingly the scandal of it, because the lie of the despot . . . will always be the flattery of the slave. . . .
>
> Russian despotism not only counts ideas and sentiments as nothing, but it remakes the facts, it struggles against the evident, and it triumphs in the cause."[19]

And now Custine, making his own observations, could only echo these views. "One must confess it," he wrote, "Russians of all classes conspire with a marvellous harmony of effort to bring about the triumph of duplicity in their country." They had "a dexterity in the use of the lie, a natural facility for falseness" which, he said, "revolted his sincerity."[20] And it seemed to him that this was, in his own words, "the most enormous of faults." Why? Because "in renouncing the truth," he explained, "the spirit abdicates, and by a strange reversal of things it is then the master who humiliates himself before the slave; for the man who deceives is beneath the man who is deceived."[21]

In one respect, however, Custine came to modify this view before his journey was ended. He had spoken, in the passage just cited, of the "man who is deceived." But he was eventually obliged to ask himself the question: was anyone really deceived? Precisely because everything was hidden, he noted, everything was also guessed: "I look in vain for the dupes of these puerile falsehoods, and I cry out to myself like Basil: Who is deceived, here? Tout le monde est dans le secret."[22]

However, if everyone was in on the secret, everyone was taking jolly good care, Custine also noted, not to show that he was; and the resulting atmosphere of total discretion— the quiet cautiousness, the wary guardedness of speech, the unwillingness to call things by their right names—was another aspect of Russian life that made the deepest sort of impression upon him. He referred to it as "the silence," and he conceived of it as a pervasive and sinister condition of Russian society. He found it symbolized by the strange, almost eerie stillness that prevailed on the Petersburg streets and public places. "In Russia," he observed, "only the horses have permission to make a noise."[23]

Here, once again, his shipboard companion had not failed to tell him what was in store for him. "However little one speaks in Russia," Prince Kozlovski had said, "one always speaks too much, because in this country every discussion is the expression of a religious or political hypocrisy."[24] And now, once again, Custine had occasion to make his own observations. In Russia, he concluded,

> secrecy presides over everything: administrative secrecy, political, social secrecy; discretion useful and discretion useless. A silence that is superfluous assures the silence that is necessary. Here, discretion is the order of the day, just as imprudence is in Paris. Every traveller is in himself an indiscretion. . . .[25]

And it dawned on him then that this silence, too, was part of the Russian inferiority complex with relation to the world outside. It was a weapon of foreign policy—a defensive weapon, a very effective one. "If it is true," he wrote, that better diplomats are to be found among the Russians than among the most advanced peoples, the reason is that our press informs the Russians about every plan that is proposed and every event that occurs among us. Instead of prudently concealing our weaknesses we reveal them every morning with passion, while the Byzantine policy of the Russians, at work in the shadows, is careful to hide what they are thinking and doing and fearing. We go forward in the light of day; they advance under cover. We are blinded by the ignorance in which they leave us; they are enlightened by our candor. We are weakened by rumor; they are strengthened by secrecy. And there you have the secret of their cleverness.[26]

And yet it occurred to Custine that all these tendencies—the disrespect for the truth, the deliberate mystification, the studied silence—while representing weapons in the hands of the regime, were also the reflections of a great underlying weakness—a weakness precisely in relation to the West. They reflected, as Custine saw it, an awareness of backwardness, a distrust of one's own people, a shame for the tyranny one dared not live without—qualities that made Russians quail at the thought of any free and true comparison with western conditions. It was this that lay at the bottom of the obsessive fear of foreign observation that seemed to him to permeate Russian officialdom.

The absurd extremism of this fear astonished Custine as it has, I think, many westerners in other ages. The Russians, Custine wrote, "are Chinese disguised; they do not like to avow their aversion to foreign observation, but if they dared to brave the reproach of barbarism, as the true Chinese do, the access to Petersburg would be as difficult for us as is the access to Pekin."[27] And he went on to identify, with pungency and brevity, the basic reason for this state of affairs. "The more I see of Russia," he wrote, "the more I approve the conduct of the Emperor in forbidding his subjects to travel, and in rendering access to his own country difficult to foreigners. The political system of Russia could not stand twenty years' free communication with the West of Europe."[28]

And why was this? Custine arrived at his own explanation. It was not that the system had no achievements to its credit. It was that its achievements, such as they were, had been purchased at too heavy a price. The system was too costly and inefficient. He saw Russia, in fact, as a country where the most grandiose efforts produced the tiniest results. And given the nature of the system, it could not, he thought, be otherwise. Despotism was, after all, composed of

> a mixture of impatience and laziness. With just a bit more patience on the part of ruling power and a bit more activity on the part of the people the same result could be obtained at a much lower cost. But what would then become of the tyranny? One would have to recognize at once that it was useless. Tyranny is the imaginary illness of the peoples [*la maladie imaginaire des peuples*]. The tyrant, disguised as a doctor, persuades them that health is not the natural state of civilized man, and the greater the danger, the more violent, of course, must be the cure. In this way, the tyrant feeds and prolongs the ailment under the pretext of curing it.[29]

And this, Custine went on to explain, was one of the reasons —perhaps the greatest reason—why one could not accept the Russian system as a model for anyone else. "Things that I admire elsewhere," he wrote,

> I hate here. . . . I find them too dearly paid for; order, patience, calmness, elegance, respectfulness, the natural and moral relations that ought to exist between those who think and those who do, in short all that gives worth and charm to well-organised societies, all that gives meaning and purpose to political institutions,

is lost and confounded here in one single sentiment—
that of fear.[30]

Russia, accordingly, had little or no value as an example
for other countries. To the extent that Custine's journey
had been inspired by a desire to find the model of a well-
ordered society that could be invoked and held up as an
alternative to the wretched philistinism and egalitarianism
of the regime of Louis Philippe in France, this idea had
now to be abandoned. "The society of the Russians, such
as they have arranged it," he concluded with a tinge of sad-
ness, "can serve only their own uses; *il faut être Russe pour
vivre en Russie.*"[31]

All these were reflections induced in Custine by the obviously intense reluctance of Russian officialdom to permit
the true image of Russian reality to become known to foreigners and to constitute a basis for comparison between
Russia and the West. But there was, he recognized, also
something even deeper and more subjective in the distaste
for the truth, the preference for the façade, the insistence
on the discreet silence, to which this officialdom was ad-
dicted. There was an unwillingness to admit, even before
one's own people, the full ugliness of Russian despotism.
Dissimulation on so vast a scale as Custine observed it in
Russia could serve, he concluded, "only to mask a profound
inhumanity; it is not the good that one takes such care to
conceal."[32] And again: "A regime whose own violence is
such that it be supported only by such means can only be
a profoundly vicious regime."[33]

In entertaining these gloomy thoughts on the nature of
Russian despotism, Custine did not fail to take account of
those qualities in the Russian peasant masses—the brutali-
zation, the sly obstinacy, the latent anarchic trends—which
called for methods of rule different from those that would
have been effective in other countries. Like many another
western visitor to Russia, beginning in the sixteenth century with one of the first permanent western diplomatic

envoys there, Herberstein,* he could not avoid asking himself to what extent the rigors of the regime constituted an unavoidable response to the nature of the people, and he was perfectly willing to recognize the psychology of the Russian masses as an extenuating circumstance. "Clemency," he observed toward the end of his journey,

> represents weakness in the approach to a people hardened by terror; nothing disarms such a people but fear; implacable severity forces it to its knees; mercy, on the contrary, causes it to raise its head; one would not know how to convince it; one can do no other than to subdue it; incapable of pride, it is not incapable of audacity; it revolts against mildness, but gives obedience to ferocity, which it mistakes for true power.[34]

But even in these bitter reflections, he could find no fully adequate justification for the behavior of the regime. If this vicious circle of brutality and counter-brutality, this "struggle of deception, of prejudices, and of inhumanity between people and sovereign," as he termed it, was ever to be overcome, someone had to take the initiative, to set the example, and this could only be the government. "It is not to say," he explained, "that one could and should govern the Russians in this day and age as one governs other European countries; I would simply like to submit that one could avoid a number of the evils if only the example of a certain softening of the customs and manners [*l'exemple de l'adoucissement des moeurs*] were to be given from above."[35] Did not, after all, the barbarity of the serf "accuse," as he put it, the corruption of the master?[36]

Custine had no illusions that the leaders of the regime would concede this *adoucissement des moeurs*. Their pres-

* See Herberstein, in his well-known *Notes upon Russia*: "It is a matter of doubt whether the brutality of the people had made the prince a tyrant, or whether the people themselves have become thus brutal and cruel through the tyranny of their prince." (Baron Sigismund von Herberstein, *Notes upon Russia, Being a Translation of the Earliest Account of that Country, Entitled "Rerum Moscovicarum Commentari,"* London, The Hakluyt Society, 1851, p. 32). Custine was familiar with Herberstein's work and himself referred to this passage.

tige was too intimately engaged in the old policies. To modify these policies now would be to admit past error. "They fear," he wrote, "the evil effects of a tardy justice, and they aggravate the evil precisely in order not to be forced to justify [past] excesses."[37]

Like many other visitors to Russia, Custine was struck by the monumentality, the preposterous scale, the vastness and enormity, of all that the government created. What, he asked himself, could all this be designed to symbolize, to commemorate? Scarcely Russia's past: this was too shallow, too unhappy. Also not the present: this was too unimpressive and depressing. Only the future remained. Undertakings so vast in scale could be justified only by service to some grandiose design—to some far-flung ambition, embracing more than past and present, and more than just Russia alone.

And what could this be? There was only one conceivable answer: world conquest—conquest in the name of ideological proselytism—conquest as a concealment and expiation of internal failure. This, he concluded, was the *"arrière-pensée"* behind all Russian policy. It was an *arrière-pensée* to which men deferred without even being aware that they were doing so. But the recognition of it seemed to him essential to any understanding of Russia. Without it, he wrote, "the history of Russia would appear to me an inexplicable enigma."[38] What, after all, was "Saint Petersburg in its magnificence and immensity" if not *"un trophée élevé par les Russes à leur puissance a venir?"*[39]

There was of course nothing new, even in Custine's day, about the idea of world conquest as the innermost impulse of Russian policy. For 350 years western travellers in Russia had been arriving at similar thoughts and suspicions. Of this, too, the Russian prince had spoken, on board the ship; and he had offered his explanation. There had been a time, he had said, when Russia had herself stood, as a Christian nation, between the Mongol hordes and the civilization of Europe. But things had now changed. Russia had herself become a semi-Asiatic country. And having been for centuries oppressed and humiliated by the Tatar hordes, Russian rulers were now inspired by a subconscious desire to compensate for these humiliations by inflicting them on others—at home and abroad. Suffering, after all, did not make people humane. It was a habit of princes and of people to take their revenge upon the innocent. They fancied themselves strong when they created victims. Thus the Russians had now come to occupy with relation to Europe the place the Mongols had once occupied with relation to Russia. The role of buffer between Europe and Asia, once filled by Russia herself, had come now to be assumed by the Poles.[40]

This point made a profound impression on Custine when he first heard it from Kozlovski's lips. And now people in Russia confirmed it. "Europe," he quotes some of them as saying to him in Petersburg, "is following the road that Poland took: she is enervating herself in a vain liberalism, whilst we continue powerful precisely because we are not free; let us be patient under the yoke; others will some day pay for our shame."[41]

The logic of this thesis, and his inability to find a better explanation for many of the phenomena with which he was faced, filled Custine with a dread sense of the menace that Russia must someday constitute for Western Europe—for a Western Europe, in particular, that seemed to be losing its faith in its own ideals and traditions. And it was to this thought that he addressed what seem to me to be some of the most eloquent and significant passages of his entire work. "An ambition inordinate and immense," he wrote,

one of those ambitions which could only possibly spring in the bosoms of the oppressed, and could find nourishment only in the miseries of an entire nation, ferments in the heart of the Russian people. That nation, essentially aggressive, greedy under the influence of privation, expiates beforehand, by a debasing submission, the design of exercizing a tyranny over other nations: the glory, the riches, which are the objects of its hopes, console it for the disgrace to which it submits. To purify himself from the foul and impious sacrifice of all public and personal liberty, the slave, sunk to his knees, dreams of world domination.[42]

Did one, Custine then asked himself, have to take these dreams seriously? What was this thought of conquest, which he now saw and described as "the secret life of Russia?"[43] "Is it merely a lure," he asked himself, "designed to seduce primitive populations over one period of time or another, or must it some day be realized?"[44] He confessed himself obsessed with this question. "Ever since I came to Russia," he wrote,

> I have taken a dark view of the future of Europe. This opinion is challenged, to be sure, by some very wise and experienced men. They maintain that I exaggerate Russian power. Every society, they say, suffers its reverses, and the destiny of this one is to expand to the East and then to become itself divided. . . .*
>
> [But] I see the Colossus from close at hand and I find it difficult to persuade myself that the only object of this creation of Providence is to diminish the barbarism of Asia. It appears to me that it is chiefly destined to chastise the corrupt civilization of Europe, by the agency of a new invasion. The eternal tyranny of the East menaces us incessantly; and we shall have to bow before it, if our extravagances and iniquities render us worthy of the punishment.[45]

To Custine, the danger of Russia's strength was always, first and foremost, a function of Europe's own weakness. "It is not for nothing," he wrote,

> that Providence is piling up these enormous inactive forces in the East of Europe. Some day this sleeping giant will rouse himself, and then force will put an end to our wordy liberal confusion [literally, to "rule by the word"]. . . .

* The contemporary reader will not fail to note the relevance of this passage to the Chinese-Soviet conflict.

When our cosmopolitan democracy, bearing its final fruit, has made out of war something odious to entire populations, when those nations that are supposed to be the most civilised ones on earth have finally enervated themselves in their political debauchery and have fallen progressively into internal somnolence and the world's contempt, when, swooning in their egotism, they have lost all attraction for others as allies, then the floodgates of the North* will be opened once more in our faces, and we shall be subjected to a final invasion, no longer by ignorant barbarians but by sophisticated, enlightened masters, masters more enlightened than ourselves, for they will have learned from our excesses how we could and should be ruled.[46]

But would this then, Custine asked himself, as many people were to ask themselves at a later period in history, would this be so terrible? Would it be the end? Would a Russian domination be really intolerable? Would it not have its uses? He did not think so. He explained, in words that recall much of the contemporary discussion of Soviet policy in Czechoslovakia, why he rejected this suggestion:

A Russian domination, even if it should limit itself to diplomatic demands, without proceeding to actual conquest, would seem to me to be the deadliest possible thing for the world. One is deceiving one's self about the role that country would play in Europe. By its own constitutional principles, Russia appears to represent order; but by the character of its people it would propagate tyranny under the pretext of putting an end to anarchy.[47]

This, then, was Custine's view of the significance of Russia for the future of Europe. A threat? Yes. Unavoidably so, because Russia's backwardness, the uneven rhythm of

---

* The term "North" was often used, at that time, to refer in a general way to Russia, as the term "East" might be today.

her own development, and her inability to come to terms with herself forbade it to be otherwise. A nation that was not at peace with itself could not be at peace with its neighbors. But the menace Russia presented was something that could be measured only in terms of Europe's own weakness.

Russia was aggressive—yes—out of a desire to be something it was not. Europe, however, was threatened primarily by its failure to be all that it really was.

Russia was aggressive—yes—for lack of a quality it recognized and envied in others but did not itself possess. Europe was threatened primarily by its failure to respect and to preserve a quality that was already its own.

Russia was a menace to itself and to others—yes—by virtue of the fact that it had no past to believe in. Europe was threatened primarily by its failure to respect the past that it had.

There were noted, at the beginning of this chapter, the views on political institutions with which Custine entered upon his journey to Russia. It remains to note the ones with which he returned, for they were different in emphasis even though they may not have been, as he himself claimed, greatly different in kind.

The reader will recall Custine's statement that he went to Russia "to seek arguments against representative government." Actually, this was only a part of the sentence. It is now necessary to take cognizance of the remainder of it, which read: "but I return the partisan of constitutions."

In other passages of the book, Custine explained in greater detail what he meant by this statement:

In France, I had imagined myself in accord with these rigourous disciplinarians; but since I have lived under a despotism which imposes military rule upon the population of an entire empire, I confess that I have learnt to prefer a little of the disorder which announces vigour to the perfect order which destroys life.[48]

I left France scared by the abuses of a false liberty; I return to my country persuaded that if, logically speaking, the representative system is not the most moral form of government, it is, practically, the most wise and moderate; preserving the people on the one side from democratic license, and on the other, from the most glaring abuses of despotism; I therefore ask myself if we ought not to impose a silence upon our antipathies, and submit without murmur to a necessary policy, and one which, after all, brings to nations prepared for it, more good than evil.[49]

It is difficult to know what value to assign to these statements. Their similarity to the conclusions arrived at only shortly before by Tocqueville on the basis of his journey to the United States is so great that one suspects Custine, as he wrote these passages, to have been strongly under Tocqueville's influence, and perhaps unconsciously anxious to gain for himself a bit of the acclaim Tocqueville had won with his book. Be that as it may, there is no doubt that these words reflected truly the feelings with which Custine completed his Russian journey. And they will stand, in any case, as classical statements of the effect which travel and residence in Russia has had on countless western visitors, in reconciling them to the imperfections of the political systems of their own native countries. For this, they need only be supplemented by the well-known sentences with which Custine ended his entire book.

To have a feeling for the liberty enjoyed in the other European countries one must have sojourned in that solitude without repose, in that prison without leisure, that is called Russia.

If ever your sons should be discontented with France, try my recipe: tell them to go to Russia. It is a journey useful to every foreigner; whoever has well examined that country will be content to live anywhere else.

So much for Custine's reactions to Russia. It is these, outstandingly, for which the book is known. But the impression given of Custine's qualities of insight and judgment would not be complete if no mention were made of certain of his judgments on broader problems of international life. The passages in which these judgments are embodied are ones which, to my knowledge, have not received attention in any of the published works concerning Custine; but they deserve notice because they too appear, like so many of the judgments concerning Russia, to leap across the intervening decades and to have an actuality in the mid-twentieth century far greater than any they could have had at the time.

In these passages, Custine entered the lists against the concepts of romantic nationalism that were becoming standard features of personality for at least three generations of coming statesmen and thinkers, not only in France but throughout the western world. Departing from a series of insights which only the bitter experience of two world wars and the spectre of the atom have been able to bring to others, he challenged the validity of the concept of national glory (to which even Tocqueville was attached); he rejected the uses of any attempt to spread power or ideology by proselytizing among other peoples; he praised the model of the small state, concentrating on the internal improvement of its own society, over that of the great state, bent on the expansion of its power; he rejected materialism, imperialism, and war, in all their forms. How it was possible for a man to arrive at ideas so wholly contrary to the entire developing atmosphere of his own century and culture remains one of the mysteries with which Custine's person and cast of mind seem always to have been surrounded. With these introductory observations, the passages in question may be permitted to speak for themselves:

However much our religious propaganda may appear to me sublime, to that same extent I find odious every sort of political proselytism—the spirit, that is, of conquest or, more precisely still, the spirit of rapine justified by an over-clever sophistry that goes by the name of glory. Far from uniting the human species, this narrow ambition only divides it.[50]

I observe, among the most civilized of the world's countries, certain states which have power only over their own subjects, who are themselves small in number. These states have no weight at all in world politics. It is not by the pride of conquest nor by the exercise of a tyrannical power over foreigners that their governments have won the right to a universal recognition; it is by their good example, by their wise laws, by an enlightened and beneficent administration. With such advantages a small people can become not the conqueror of the world, but rather its torch-bearer, which is a hundred times preferable. . . . In our country the fascination with war and conquest continues to endure, despite the lessons of the god of heaven, and despite—also—those of the god of the earth, which is self-interest. . . .

I hope to live long enough to see the shattering of this bloody idol of war and brute force. One's power and one's territory are always sufficient to one's purpose if one has the courage to live and die for the truth, if one pursues error to the bitter end, if one sheds one's blood for the destruction of falsehood and injustice.

It is not by looking covetously to the outside that peoples establish their right to universal recognition, it is by directing their energy upon themselves and becoming what they can become under the double influence of spiritual and material civilization. This species of merit is as superior to the propaganda of the sword as virtue is preferable to glory.

That super-annuated expression: "a power of the first order" as it is applied to national policy, will be for a long time to come the source of the unhappiness of the world.[51]

VI. *THE REACTION TO*
RUSSIA IN 1839

Custine's book about Russia finally saw publication in May 1843—nearly four years after Custine entered upon the journey that gave rise to it. As stated at the outset of this account, it was an immediate, and indeed most astonishing, success. Amyot, the official publisher, disposed of four editions in the course of three years. The Brussels *"contrafacteurs"* (as Custine termed them)—the Société Typographique Belge—appear to have put out four of their several editions before Amyot had even come to the second one. (These, incidentally, were direct copies of the first edition, but of much smaller format—so small, in fact, that one marvels that people were able to read them.) The English, German, and Danish translations followed with what was, considering the length of the work and the non-existence of the typewriter, amazing promptitude. Within two or three years after the initial publication, Custine was able to estimate that the total sales had run into at least 200,000 copies. This popular success was all the more remarkable by the virtue of the fact that it appears to have had little or no relationship to the reviews which the book received.*

The reception of the book by the periodical press was complicated by a number of factors. First of all, in the country where the most qualified reviewers might have been found

---

* Custine, in fact, with his delicate wit, attributed the popularity of the first edition partly to the fact that the leading Paris editors had failed to review it.

—namely, Russia itself—the importation, sale, and public discussion of the book were all officially prohibited. There could, therefore, be no reviews in Russian journals. The reaction of the educated public in Russia can be judged only from the odd passages in letters, or quotations of oral observations by one person or another, that have come down to us in the historical record. Going by this evidence, one must conclude that it was a very rare Russian indeed who was not irritated or to some degree negatively affected by the reading of the work. The book, obviously, was a mixture of things that were sufficiently inaccurate to be annoying (mostly matters of detailed fact) and ones that were sufficiently true to hurt. It is hard to tell which of these caused the greater discontent. But precisely because those points that were true, or were well-observed, tended to be things the Russians disliked to recognize in themselves or their country, it was the others—the inaccuracies—to which they normally drew attention as a means of expressing their discontent. For a Russian, Custine's book was both irritating in its general tenor and vulnerable to refutation in detail. The private Russian responses reflected both these qualities.

Although the editor's preface to the second edition claimed that the Russian border formalities had been considerably improved as a result of Custine's sardonic description of them, the book seems to have had very little effect, if any, on the general behavior of the regime or the development of Russian society. So strong was the official disapproval that it became quite unthinkable to cite Custine as a reason for this or that change, this or that reform, in Russian officialdom or Russian society. This, no doubt, is what was reflected in one of the soundest and most perceptive of the private Russian reactions that have come down to us. It came from the sister-in-law of the Emperor and second lady of the land, the Grand Duchess Hélène, protectress and patroness of Kozlovski, and very much a woman of parts. While taking the cure in Germany, in the summer of 1843, she met Custine's friend Varnhagen von Ense. He, in a letter of July 31, 1843, quoted her as observing that Custine had exaggerated quite considerably all that was bad in Russia and had often appeared not to see that which was good. "She admits," he went on, "that on a number of points he was right, but that instead of improving people he only embittered and shocked them. . . . Certainly, his book would have an effect; but a more calm and less impassioned *tableau* would have had an even stronger one."[1]

In Western Europe, there were not many people, if any, who knew enough about Russia to measure the picture that emerged from Custine's account against the realities of that great country. Slavic studies had not at that time advanced far enough to occupy a place of any importance in the concerns of the western scholarly community. There were no "experts" on Russia in the modern sense of the term. There were indeed people who had, at one time or another, lived in Russia, and even more who had travelled there; but not many of these people were of such intellectual calibre that they could enter the literary lists with Custine; and of the travellers, few had remained longer, or viewed the country in greater depth, than Custine himself. Recent travellers in Russia tended to be people who had either written accounts of their experiences there or wished they had, who were jealous of Custine for the success of his book, and who were inclined for this reason to denigrate it, convinced that they, had they wished, could have written a much better one.

When it came to France itself, which was after all the country of publication, the reviewing was affected by a number of factors unrelated to the merits of the work. There was the commitment of various journals to this or that position of French foreign policy, particularly policy towards Russia. The venality of the French press being what it then was, there was the factor of what one might call "purchased distortion," the Russian government being not the least among the purchasers. Finally, there was the personal reaction of editors and reviewers to Custine himself.

He was a man who had few good friends, many detractors, and not a few enemies, particularly among the critics. He was, as he himself on one occasion admitted, a person whom one loved "better from afar than from nearby."[2] The combination, furthermore, of his reputed great wealth, his literary ambitions, and his reputation for willingness to finance the favorable reviewing of his own literary works, tended actually to put the editors on their guard against the printing of anything very favorable about things he wrote, lest they be suspected of being in his pay. (There is on record one instance in which a publisher confessed to Balzac that, precisely for this reason, he had caused one of Custine's works to be reviewed less favorably than it deserved.)

In the face of all these considerations it was scarcely to be expected that the appearance of *La Russie en 1839* would evoke any very thoughtful, penetrating or fair evaluation in the western press.

For whatever reasons—and these presumably included the length of the book, the delicacy of the subject, the difficulty of finding qualified reviewers (perhaps also a certain habitual underestimation of Custine)—the Paris editors were slow in responding to the appearance of *La Russie en 1839*.* The first serious reviews did not appear before the end of the year 1843, by which time the Brussels publishers were already roaring along with their various editions, and even the leisurely Amyot was busy, with Custine's collaboration, in the preparation of a second one. But this does not mean that there had been no printed reactions at all. Russians everywhere, reading the work over the summer of 1843, were stung to the quick by the sharpness of the attack; and several of them, not being able to review the work for the Russian public, hastened to do what they could to weaken

---

* I must acknowledge that in the preparation of this chapter, in particular, I have done little more than to follow to their ends, where I could, the trails so conscientiously blazed by M. Cadot. I can only thank him for his pains in uncovering them, and confirm that I never found his accounts of what lay at their ends to be otherwise than scrupulously accurate.

its effect on the public of western European countries. The result was the appearance in Western Europe, in the winter of 1843-44, of a series of pamphlets or articles, mostly anonymous, attacking Custine's account. These have often been viewed as inspired and financed by the Russian government; and indeed the three most important of them were written by men who in fact stood in one or another sort of relationship to the Russian government. One of these was the grammarian, N. I. Grech, whose presence as a co-passenger of Custine on the *Nicholas I* has already been noted (Chapter III, above). The second was a Russian diplomat of Polish origin by the name of Xavier Labenski. In private life a man of letters (he wrote poetry in French and seems to have regarded himself as part of the French cultural community), Labenski was at that time serving in the Foreign Office in St. Petersburg.

The third of these semi-official reactions came from a fairly well-known Russian literary figure, then resident in Paris: Yakov Nikolayevich Tolstoi.* At one time a liberal idealist and moderately involved in the Decembrist conspiracy, Tolstoi had been obliged to go into exile after the insurrection. He lived for long in Paris in the status—initially, no doubt, genuine—of a political refugee. In the 1830's, however, his relationship with the Tsarist authorities underwent a quiet alteration, and he was recruited as an agent of the Russian secret police, with the cover-title of a "correspondent" of the Russian Ministry of Education,† to serve primarily as a clandestine channel for the exertion of influence over the French press.‡ His former political

---

* Not, of course, to be confused with the great writer of that name, Lev Tolstoi, then only a child.

† Tolstoi's overt duties as a Correspondent for the Ministry of Education related to the procurement of historical documents from the French archives. In this respect they bore a close resemblance to the occupation of Alexander Turgenev; and indeed, when Turgenev finally left Paris, in 1844, a certain portion of the work he had been doing there was turned over to Tolstoi for completion.

‡ It is amusing, in the light of what is now known about Tolstoi's police connections, to read, in his attack on Custine's book, his own description of a spy. After criticizing Custine for referring to certain

connections permitted him to pose as a liberal and in this way to enjoy a certain sort of confidence among numbers of people who would certainly not have extended it to him had they even suspected that he was serving the Russian government. (His cover was not seriously compromised until 1846, when an indiscretion on the part of one of the police officials in Petersburg caused difficulties for him in Paris.)

These three semi-official Russian critics all struck similar notes. They picked Custine up on his many inaccuracies. They exposed his inconsistencies. They charged him with tactlessness and ingratitude. They held him up to ridicule for the personal anxieties he confessed to having experienced on his journey, and—in some instances—for his unsavory reputation.

Grech's pamphlet, published under his own name, was entitled *Examen de l'ouvrage de M. le marquis de Custine intitulé "La Russie en 1839."* Originally written in Russian, it appeared in German translation in Heidelberg, and in French translation in Brussels (Imprimerie de Politique), in January 1844.* Grech pronounced Custine's book "a tissue of lies, inaccuracies, blunders, contradictions, and slanders." Custine, he charged, had not understood Russia; he had not wanted to understand it; he had judged it, in fact, "as a deaf-mute might judge the performance of an opera."

---

of the Russian officials as "spies," and pointing out, quite rightly, that one who functions overtly as a servant of his government could not properly be given that designation, he went on:

A spy, Sir, is a man who disguises his intentions, who dons the mask of an honest man to win confidence, who stoops to pick up the things others have left carelessly behind, and who spices his reports in order to give himself importance and to elevate his ignoble occupation. Princes, and the public, sometimes make use of such people and derive amusement from their pretended revelations; but they are never given esteem.[3]

One senses from this passage, written only a year before his own cover was blown, that poor Tolstoi had scant satisfaction from his relationship with the Russian police.

* A copy of Grech's pamphlet, the only one known to me to exist in the United States, can be seen in the New York Public Library.

Tolstoi's contribution, imitating Custine's own form of obviously spurious "letters," was entitled: *"La Russie en 1839" rêvée par M. de Custine ou lettres sur cet ouvrage écrites de Francfort.* It appeared over the pseudonym of J. Yakovlev. As in the case of Grech's piece, a German edition appeared in 1844 in Leipzig, and a French edition was put out almost simultaneously, with no designation of publisher, the place for such designation being pre-empted by the curious phrase: *"Chez les principaux libraires."*

Tolstoi's attack, the most personal of the three, was more satirical and more malicious than the others, and obviously designed to destroy Custine by sheer ridicule rather than by the exposure of individual inaccuracies. Like Grech, Tolstoi was unable to resist the exploitation of Custine's reputation as a homosexual; and his passage on this point, which even included a specific reference to the 1824 incident (now two decades in the past), was the crueler of the two. While admitting that there were individual passages in Custine's book "touched with grace and talent," Tolstoi nevertheless pronounced the book to be the "work of a false spirit and evil heart." It had been written, he alleged, with malevolent intent—with a view to burying under a new sensationalism the memory of "a certain scandalous adventure." Russians might deem themselves fortunate that a man so hostile could find nothing else with which to attack them but the lie and calumny.

The pamphlet of Labenski, the diplomat, also appeared anonymously (it was signed simply: "Un Russe"). It was entitled: *Un Mot sur l'ouvrage de M. le marquis de Custine intitulé "La Russie en 1839."* An English translation (London, T. C. Newby, 1844) followed almost immediately, un-

---

* The Widener Library, at Harvard University, has copies of both the French and German editions of this work. It is a curious fact that both Grech and Tolstoi went out of their way to convey the impression that their articles had been written in Frankfurt and in the Russian language, that the initial publication was in German, and that the publication of a French translation was an afterthought. The reader may arrive at his own guess at the reasons for this subterfuge.

der the editorship of one Henry J. Bradfield, who wrote for the volume an introduction in no way inferior to the remainder of the book in the bitterness of its attack on Custine.

Labenski's monograph was the most dignified and serious of the three, and the best-written. He, like Tolstoi, refrained from wasting his breath on the detailed refutation of individual errors and devoted himself to demolishing Custine by ridicule; but his prose was better, his tone more relaxed, and his approach more suave and effective, than in the case of the others.

These three pamphlets have often been viewed as inspired and financed by the Russian government. Actually, things were not quite this way. While Tolstoi does indeed seem to have been reimbursed by the police in Petersburg for what he claimed were the expenses of his effort, and while Grech had high hopes of being similarly rewarded,* the initiative for the monographs seems to have come primarily from the authors themselves. The Russian government, after some reflection, evidently decided, in fact, that the less Custine's book was talked about, the better.† In a letter addressed by one of the senior police officials to Grech it was said, and surely on high authority, that the Russian government saw no reason why Russian writers should not voluntarily assume the task of defending their country, as the writers of other countries did, against literary calumnies from abroad. "To seek out such writers and to have them under its influence," it was said, "would not be fitting to the dignity of our government, which is no less inclined than ever to direct its attention, with gratitude, to

* Grech damaged, if he did not destroy, his chances for remuneration by his own indiscretions, as a result of which a story appeared in a German paper to the effect that he had been charged by the Russian government with the preparation of a refutation of Custine. This drew down upon him, instead of the reward he expected, a severe reprimand from Petersburg.

† Labenski's pamphlet appears even to have been held up by Russian customs, on shipment to Russia. Alexander Turgenev professed himself bewildered by this action. "But the argument is on our side," he complained, in a letter to Bulgakov.

writers who labor on their own initiative for its interests, but cannot and should not be involved in the matter, lest it show itself in need of defenders."[4]

All of these pamphlets were fairly widely read (Tolstoi's the least so) and they were not wholly without effect. Labenski's, in particular, published in England as a separate book, had a perceptible effect, as will be seen, on the reviewers as well as directly on the public there.* But by and large, these pamphlets were too obviously partisan, and the signs of their semi-official origin too strong, for them to have any decisive effect on the public reception of the book. It is significant that Alexander Turgenev, laying down Grech's work after the first reading, sighed (figuratively, in one of his letters to Bulgakov) over the fact that Custine had not yet been confronted with "a business-like and clean critic."[5]

Among the major French reviews, which began to appear only at the end of 1843, the unfavorable ones predominated. One of these appeared in *La Presse*, the organ of the great but unscrupulous founder of the "boulevard" press, Émile de Girardin.

The Russian police archives have a good deal to say about Girardin, and it is evident that for years on end he received encouragement, if not subsidies, from that quarter for an editorial policy that was consistently pro-Russian. Yakov Tolstoi, in taking over his position as a clandestine Russian agent in Paris in the late 1830's, named *La Presse*, in a dispatch to his superiors in the Russian police, as one of the papers that could assuredly be influenced by discreet financial support. The archives also reveal, to be sure, that by 1843 the officials of the Third Section were a bit leery of Girardin, regarding him as a shady and untrustworthy character, in whose discretion no proper confidence could

---

* Labenski's monograph was also incorporated into the fifth of the pirated editions put out (this one in 1844) by the Société Typographique Belge, and was thus available to all readers of that edition of Custine's work.

be placed. They were even careful to keep on file certain of his communications to them that could be effectively used to blackmail him in case he should prove too much of an embarrassment. They continued, nevertheless, to toy with him; and he continued, whether in gratitude for subsidies already received or in hopes of receiving future ones, to take his pro-Russian line.* One cannot, in these circumstances, regard the unfavorable review that appeared in *La Presse* as entirely disinterested.

The scathing review that appeared in the *Revue de Paris* from the pen of the young poet, J. Chaudes-Aigues, is harder to explain. Here, the attacks on Custine were highly personal, and cruel. He was even ridiculed for his earlier and less successful literary works. Custine's book, Chaudes-Aigues wrote, belonged to the genre of *la littérature confidentielle*; this could indeed have charm, but only when it came from *un homme illustre*. "Est-on illustre," he asked rhetorically, "pour avoir écrit des romans tels qu'Aloys . . ." etc.? After this opening note, the attack was pressed throughout primarily against the literary qualities of Custine's work. Much of what Custine had written was, Chaudes-Aigues charged, borrowed from other and better writers. The political and religious ideas brought forward in the book were confused and childish. Altogether, it amounted to nothing more than "a diffuse pamphlet, devoid of significance."[6]

Chaudes-Aigues was, of course, a respectable literary figure; and it is scarcely plausible that he should have put his name to anything written by anyone else. Nevertheless one is intrigued to find, in a despatch from the Russian ambassador in Paris to his foreign minister, Count Nesselrode, of July 1843, the following curious passage: "Pursuant to certain steps I have taken, the refutation of the book of

---

* It is interesting to find Émile de Girardin nearly forty years later, at the end of his long career as publicist and editor, placing his paper of that day, the *Gaulois*, at the service of the implacable French chauvinist, Madame Juliette Adam, in her effort to prod a reluctant French government into the conclusion of an alliance with Russia. Were the Russian coffers, one wonders, continuing to flow?

M. de Custine which has been sent to me should appear first in the *Revue de Paris*, then in the *feuilleton* or the supplement to the *Quotidienne*."[7] It will be most charitable to assume that Chaudes-Aigues simply took into account, in writing his own review, whatever material had been sent to the *Revue de Paris* from the Russian Embassy. It is evident, in any case, that the Russian authorities, while not anxious to have Russians write refutations, were not averse to attempting to influence the French reviewers.

These unfavorable reviews were perhaps balanced, in Custine's eyes at least, by two relatively favorable ones that appeared in the *Journal des Débats*. These were from the pen of another and quite different Girardin—Saint-Marc Girardin, critic and professor of literature, already known as a defender of the Polish cause. His selection as a reviewer no doubt reflected the political line of the paper, which had long been opposed to the idea of a Franco-Russian alignment. The *Journal* is said, however, to have been the only French paper which the Russian Emperor regularly read; and for this reason, as well as by virtue of its semi-official status, a special importance attaches to its treatment of Custine.

As analyses of Custine's book, Saint-Marc Girardin's articles were not appreciably more profound than those of the hostile critics. In the first of them, which appeared on January 4, 1844, he concentrated on the difficulties encountered by any foreign visitor in Russia desirous of forming a close acquaintance with the Russian scene. Summarizing, and partly quoting, certain of Custine's passages, he produced two paragraphs which, as descriptions of the visitor's dilemma, have a certain classic quality in themselves.* And he

* These observations of Custine's, as summarized by Saint-Marc Girardin, deserve to be rescued from obscurity. Here they are:

What is most difficult in Russia is to see anything through one's own eyes. Are you in even the smallest degree a privileged traveller? You are then accompanied everywhere, as a means of controlling what you see. Do you wish to see a palace? You will be given a chamberlain who will do you the honors from top to bottom. Do you wish to go through a military camp? An officer, went on to ridicule the various anonymous, or officially-inspired, pamphlets that Custine's book had evoked, particularly for the absurdity of the attempt to explain away the Lübeck innkeeper's observations by the phenomenon of seasickness. The second article was really a refutation of the pamphlet of Grech, rather than a review of Custine's work. Saint-Marc Girardin picked Grech up on his rather absurd defense of the Russian censorship, on the injustice of his charge that Custine had spoken ill of the Emperor, and finally, once again (none of them seemed to be able to leave this alone), on the inexhaustible topic of the reasons for the appearance of Russian passengers boarding or leaving the *Nicholas I.*

An interesting side effect of Saint-Marc Girardin's articles was to provoke what was probably the best of all the negative appraisals of Custine's book, but one that remained, unfortunately, both incomplete and unpublished. M. Cadot discovered in the Moscow State Archives, and published for the first time (as an annex to his chapter on the public

---

sometimes a general, will accompany you. A hospital? The doctor-in-chief will escort you. A fortress? The commandant will show it to you, or rather he will conceal it politely. A school? A public establishment? The director or the inspector will be warned of your visit; you will find them armed for the purpose. . . . This is the fate of the *voyageurs protégés*. But the others? The others see nothing. No door opens otherwise than with permission and authorization, so that it is impossible to see Russia *dans son déshabillé*. . . . Russia is always in uniform or at present-arms when she receives you; either that, or you aren't worth for her the trouble of getting dressed up, in which case her door is closed.

. . . it is necessary to mention also the spy who is attached to every traveller, noble or otherwise, suspected of being curious. The spy is the obligatory shadow of the traveller who writes. Actually, he is not uncomfortable or embarrassing; he is eager, industrious, thoughtful; he performs all sorts of petty services which one may accept without being bound to gratitude; he is your tourist guide; he points out the curiosities of the palace; he tells you anecdotes. . . . But if you have a kind soul, don't question him too much. "The spy," M. de Custine says very well, "believes only in espionage, and if you escape his snares, he imagines that he is going to fall into yours."

reception of *La Russie en 1839*), a holograph of some thirty-three pages from the pen of none other than Vyazemski, entitled: *Encore quelques mots sur l'ouvrage de M. de Custine: "La Russie en 1839," à propos de l'article du Journal des Débats, du 4 janvier 1844.*[8]

Both the background of this literary effort and the reasons for Vyazemski's failure to complete and publish it are obscure.* Turgenev had written him, as early as August 1843, renewing an earlier plea to let him have an opinion on Custine's work. Vyazemski had evidently ignored this plea, and even the renewed request seems not to have elicited any response, for as late as December Turgenev was continuing to complain to Bulgakov: "He [Vyazemski] must have some reason for his silence; but I, so far as I know, have given him no such reason, for I love him as much as ever, although we are just as far apart in our opinions as we have been over this recent period."[9]

It was not only to Turgenev that the idea occurred of getting Vyazemski's opinion on the book. In a letter to Vyazemski of April 27, 1844, Turgenev quoted the elderly poet, Vasili Andreyevich Zhukovski (presumably then in Paris) as saying:

> If that hypocritical blabber-mouth [Custine] puts out a new edition of his pasquil in four volumes, then Vyazemski must take hold of the matter and respond; but the response must be short; it must be directed not against the book, for there is a lot of truth in it, but against Custine: in short, the response must be simply a printed punishment (he is clever, this Zhukovski, don't you think?) in anticipation of a material punishment. . . . I won't venture to comment on what Zhukovski has said; if you prefer not to follow his advice, don't do so.[10]

Actually, however, Vyazemski had obviously reached for his pen before this last letter was received; and the result

* M. Cadot thinks the government discouraged publication of the piece.

was the manuscript which M. Cadot unearthed and brought for the first time to public attention.

Vyazemski's piece, as left in its unfinished state, had its faults. The author got carried away at times with denunciations of the parliamentary regime in France, and of the French press—denunciations with which, one suspects, Custine would have heartily agreed. In general, he made liberal use, as did the anti-Custine pamphleteers, of the *tu quoque* argument—who are you in Western Europe to be criticizing Russia? Look at yourselves—an argument that was hardly germane to Custine's case. Like Chaudes-Aigues, he could not resist jeers at the mediocre success of Custine's earlier works; nor could he resist the temptation to devote several paragraphs to the inaccuracies in Custine's statements about the good ship *Nicholas I*—faults of which Custine was no doubt richly guilty but which, again, were peripheral to his basic argument. Finally, Vyazemski charged that all Custine really had to say to his readers about Russia was: (1) that it was governed by an absolute monarchy; (2) that a large proportion of the Russian peasants were in a state of serfdom; and (3) that there were courtiers in Russia.* This, surely, was a serious distortion of the tenor of Custine's work, which carried messages much more subtle and penetrating and challenging than these.

Yet Vyazemski's article, for all its faults, was in many respects the best-written and the strongest of the Russian attacks on Custine. It is a pity that it was not published, for nowhere else was the reaction of the Russian literary intelligentsia better and more authoritatively expressed.

In England, two major reviews appeared, both unfavorable. The poet and politician Richard Monckton Milnes wrote a long anonymous article for the *Edinburgh Review*. It treated, significantly, not Custine's book alone but also the pamphlet of Labenski, mentioned above, entitled *Un Mot sur l'ouvrage*, etc.; as well as another, less important one,

---

* See above, page 60, for Custine's offensive reference to Vyazemski as a "courtier." Obviously, this slight still rankled.

Edinburgh Review, 79 (April 1844), pp 351–396

by a certain M. A. Yermolov, entitled *Encore quelques mots sur l'ouvrage de M. de Custine "La Russie en 1839" par M****.

Milnes was a man of parts, and his long review was by no means without merit. It must be said to his credit that he was no less severe in his judgment on the authors of the anti-Custine pamphlets than he was on Custine. Much of what he had to say about Custine was well taken. Characteristic, perhaps, of his judgment, is the following passage:

> His sensibility is, no doubt, very excitable, and in most cases very much out of place: he is a theorist and generalizer of the wildest character; he is totally deficient in the critical faculty, and, so far, his facts are little to be relied on. But we cannot see any reason to believe him guilty of wilful misrepresentation or obstinate neglect of such truths as lay before him. He is sincere, although his sincerity may not be of the purest stamp— he is earnest, though his earnestness may be affected by self-conceit—he is fair, in so far as fairness consists in giving us the separate impressions, as they successively passed across his mind.[11]

On the other hand, Milnes' article, like most of the adverse criticisms, was in some respects unjust. He appropriated from Labenski's pamphlet the reproach to Custine for being indiscreet in recounting the statements of the Russian prince on the ship, both he and Labenski being obviously ignorant either of the identity of the prince or of the fact that he was now dead. Custine, he charged further, should have known in advance that Russia would not appeal to his aristocratic prejudices against a despotic government and to "his Catholic dislike of an Erastian heresy," and therefore should not have gone to Russia at all—an unusual proposition, when one stops to think of it, suggesting as it does that only those should travel with the thought of recording their experiences who are sure that they are prepared in advance to admire the countries they visit. Finally, Milnes' review was affected by what one suspects to have been a slight sense of jealousy and irritation over the success of Custine's work. He, himself a writer of note, had just recently visited Constantinople. He was full, one senses, of his own journey, and evidently convinced that his own observations of the East had been more objective, more profound, and more worthy of public attention than Custine's observations of Russia. A good portion of his article consisted in rather ill-tempered criticism of Custine for calling attention to deficiencies in Russian society and government which he should, in Milnes' view, have known to be simply characteristics of Oriental society generally.

The other major English review is the one that appeared, also anonymously, in the *Quarterly Review*. We owe to M. Cadot's careful and persistent researches the knowledge that this piece was probably from the pen of the writer and geologist Sir Roderick Impey Murchison, who, having studied geology in Russia in 1839, had no doubt seen far more of the off-the-beaten-path Russia than had Custine.[12] The judgment, interspersed with long quotations from some of Custine's spicier (and less accurate) anecdotes, was not unkind but also not favorable. Custine, it was said, "as a man accustomed to shine in salons, wags his pen as he would his tongue, always for effect, and more eager after point than truth." It was not every day, to be sure, that one encountered either in England or in France "volumes so entertaining and instructive"; but this circumstance did not really redeem the work. "All that is really matter of fact and observation has been told before, whilst all that is speculation may be well dispensed with."[13]

One has, in these last words, the epitome of the Victorian reaction to Custine—a reaction that explains the almost immediate disappearance of the book, after the flurry of its initial publication, from the attention of the English and American public. It is clear that what the Victorian reader looked for, in this kind of a book, was, as the anonymous reviewer expressed it, "fact and observation." The philosophic and political insights—the features that give the work its greatest interest for mid-twentieth century readers —fell utterly without resonance on Victorian susceptibilities.

An analysis of the reasons for this phenomenon would more properly be a task for the historian of late nineteenth-century thought than for the critic of Custine. One must suppose the explanation to lie in those peculiarities of temperament that caused the Victorian reader to turn his back on so much of the taste and thought of the eighteenth century, to which Custine really belonged, as on something dated and largely invalid, no longer relevant to the dawning age of material progress.

I have not been able to find any reviews of *La Russie en 1839* in American journals from the period of its initial appearance. The Crimean War, however, stirred the American reading public to a greater interest in Russia, and the work was then republished (the text being taken directly from the British Longman edition) by Appleton and Company, of New York. It was then reviewed (together with a book by Ignace de Gurowski's brother Adam and another entitled "The English Woman in Russia") in the *Southern Quarterly Review* of July 1855. The review, unsigned, was obviously written by a person of real intellectual and literary ability—not necessarily an American, for the magazine seems then to have been a joint Anglo-American venture. This writer used the occasion, however, less to discuss Custine's book than to expound some remarkably sound and prophetic views of his own with relation to the Crimean War and its setting in international politics; and while the review would be noteworthy in these connections, it is not so in the one to which this study is addressed.

By and large, then, the journalistic and literary criticism of *La Russie en 1839* was severe; and with relation to those aspects of the book that interested particularly the reviewers of that time it was not unjustly so. It was primarily the inconsistencies and inaccuracies at which the critics bridled; and these were indeed present in abundance.

Custine had his answer to both these criticisms. The charge of inconsistency was one he had anticipated in the writing of his book. "Don't reproach me for my inconsistencies," he said to the imaginary recipient of his imaginary letters, "I have perceived them before you did, without experiencing any desire to avoid them; for they are in the nature of things. If I were less sincere, I should appear to you to be more consistent."[14]

What can one say to this? What historian, in particular, faced with the contradictory quality of most historical evidence (and Russia, one should remember, is the classic country of contradictions), has not had to face the temptation to improve the coherence and persuasiveness of his account by ignoring or softening the contradictory nature of the material he has before him? The critics were right to draw attention to the contradictions; but surely a defense as candid and perceptive as this one deserved mention, too.

To the charge of inaccuracy of detail, Custine was extremely sensitive. This charge, too, he had anticipated in the writing of his book. The Russian would say, he predicted: "'Trois mois de voyage, il a mal vu.' Il est vrai, j'ai mal vu, mais j'ai bien deviné."* [15] Custine, in other words, admitted the inaccuracies but took refuge behind the insights.

Both views were of course right. Custine had indeed been guilty of the inaccuracies. But if there is any single and serious fault that could be laid at the feet of his contemporary critics, it was that in their preoccupation with the inaccuracies they ignored the insights, which were the most important aspects of the book. Custine had drawn attention, after all, to a grievous measure of discord existing between

---

* I have given these passages in the French original because they were sometimes misinterpreted and mistranslated. Milnes, for example, quoted Custine as saying that "of course he did not see much but he has guessed a good deal"; and he followed this with the crack that "indeed he has guessed nearly four volumes." Presumably, this wording, a very inadequate rendering of the original "deviné," was Milnes' own. The Longman edition, as published by Appleton in New York in 1854, contained a much less excusable, in fact almost incredible, mistranslation. Here the phrase was rendered as: "It is true I have not fully seen, but I have well defined"—"defined" being presumably some sort of grotesque transliteration of "deviné."

the pretensions attached by Russian society and its rulers to the Russian political and social system of that day and the realities that underlay it, and to the possibility that this tendency to self-deception was not just the product of lapses and errors on the part of the regime then in power but rather something deeply imbedded in the experiences of the Russian people and pregnant with disturbing implications for the future of the Russian people as a state. He had raised a serious, and, as subsequent history has proved, an enduring challenge to the concept entertained by Russian officialdom and many other educated Russians of the very nature of their own country. The task of literary criticism was not only to point out the many inaccuracies and contradictions of detail by which Custine's view of Russia was marred (although it was right that these, too, should be known) but also to examine into the justice and the implications of his major theses. This, by and large, the contemporary critics failed to do.

Among the various reactions to Custine's book there remains to be noted that of the man who, more than any other among Custine's Russian acquaintances, had taken a proprietary interest in his journey, namely, Alexander Turgenev.

Turgenev, at the moment of appearance of Custine's book (mid-May 1843) was in Russia. By odd chance, he had been abruptly summoned, on April 12, to account personally to the head of the police, and through him to the Tsar, for his part in the appearance in Paris of a book that had aroused the Tsar's anger. This was not, however, as it seems, Custine's book (although the unfavorable nature of the latter was already generally known to the Russian authorities) but one written by a young nobleman, Prince P. V. Dolgorukov, to whom Turgenev was suspected of having given certain compromising documents. Turgenev obeyed the summons to Petersburg, tendered his explanations, and was exonerated. Prince Dolgorukov, likewise summoned home from Paris, rashly obeyed the summons, was arrested on arrival, and was eventually exiled to the provinces.*

Turgenev must have learned, while in Russia, of the appearance of Custine's book; and copies of some of the earlier volumes presumably reached him there. Was he questioned about Custine's book, as well? Was his part in promoting Custine's journey known, in fact, to the Russian authorities? We do not know. Tolstoi, the Tsarist undercoverman in Paris, noted, in his attack on Custine's book, that Custine arrived in Russia with "his pockets full" of letters of introduction and that he concealed from the authorities all except the ones addressed to his banking connections.† Tolstoi, in substantiation of this statement, could point to Custine's own account (see Chapter IV, note on page 56). But was this all he knew about it? Tolstoi and Turgenev, having a similar past and now engaged in similar activities, were very well aware of each other's presence and activity in Paris. It is clear from other evidence that there was no love lost between them, and one cannot doubt that Tolstoi's curiosity to learn the identity of the writers and addressees of these letters was intense. The question, however, remains unanswered.

By midsummer, Turgenev was back in Europe—in Marienbad, to be exact. On August 10, a Russian acquaintance was bringing him the fourth volume of the "Belgian Custine," and he was trying to get copies of it to Bulgakov, and to Vyazemski.[16] Ten days later, on August 21, still in Marienbad, he was writing to Vyazemski as follows:

> For goodness' sake, answer me about Custine. (*Réponds-moi donc sur Custine.*) I shall try to make him

---

* Among the tantalizing loose ends of this account, perhaps significant, perhaps fortuitous, is the fact that Prince Dolgorukov, too, appears to have been a fellow-passenger with Custine on the *Nicholas I*. And it was in Vyazemski's house, and apparently at the time of Custine's visit to Petersburg, that the documents in question passed from Turgenev to Dolgorukov.

† The letter to Vyazemski was obviously not the only personal letter of introduction Custine had.

listen to reason on your account.* The book is being
read throughout all of Europe. I beg of you: write me
your opinion—not about the statements of fact, for
which—as such—one can only have contempt, but
about the matters of principle and the impressions,
which are expressed there without circumlocution.[17]

For the next four or five months Turgenev's correspondence was replete with references to Custine's book. He
despatched faithfully to his friends all the reviews, and all
the attacks on the book, that came his way. On December
24, he wrote (to Bulgakov):

> Yesterday they brought me a new pamphlet: *Encore
> quelques mots sur Custine*—forty pages. I do not know
> the author.† He, too, strikes out at your vile Custine
> and even defends the *chin*.‡ He doesn't touch on the
> main questions, but comes down hard rather on the
> subject of Peter I and on others of Custine's exaggera-
> tions, reproaching him also for violation of the rules
> of hospitality: the best reply would be someone's wit-
> ticism *"on aurait du lui montrer le dos; ça lui aurait
> fait plaisir."*[18]

These reactions bring up once more the puzzling question
of Turgenev's relationship to Custine and his journey. Let
us, at the cost of a slight digression, review the evidence.
Turgenev, having known Custine for some years in Paris—
at least as a casual acquaintance, meets him in June 1839,
in Frankfurt and again shortly thereafter in Kissingen, as
Custine is leaving for Russia, and gives him a letter of introduction to his, Turgenev's, most intimate friends there,

---

* This presumably referred to Vyazemski's effort to cause Custine
to remove from further editions the reference to him as a "courtier."
† This was the pamphlet by M. A. Yermolov mentioned above (p.
109). Yermolov was a Russian scholar and translator with many personal ties to the French cultural world.
‡ Chin—the order of ranks, established by Peter the Great, on
which the Russian official services, military and civil, were then still
based.

mostly men enjoying a somewhat tangled relationship to the existing Russian regime. (Custine later conceals these meetings with Turgenev, when he writes his book; and neither of the men refers, in later years, to this letter of introduction.) After their meetings in Frankfurt and Kissingen, both men proceed to Russia, but by different routes. They meet some weeks later, in distinctly odd circumstances, at the postal station by the Troitse-Sergievskaya monastery, Custine having decided only suddenly, the day before, to take that particular route from Moscow eastwards, and Turgenev, now travelling in some haste, having left Moscow shortly after Custine did. It is clear that Custine suspects Turgenev of having been sent as a courier to warn others of his, Custine's, approach. The two men have, on the occasion of this brief meeting at the postal station, a bitter argument, partly over Poland, from Custine's account of which it is clear that their relations are now both personally and politically troubled. And it seems, from the tenor of the exchange, unlikely that this is the first time they have met since they came to Russia.

Four years later, Custine's book appears. Turgenev now has no good word to say for the author. He is now "your vile Custine." It would have been better for people in Russia, he says, to have turned their backs on him (a strange suggestion, coming from one who had recommended Custine to the hospitality of a number of his own friends). Turgenev now falls in with the prevailing tone of Russian officialdom: the attacks on Custine are described as being "on our side"; he agrees that from the factual standpoint Custine's account must be regarded as beneath contempt. Yet he cannot refrain from prodding his friend Vyazemski to say what he thinks about the broader judgments with which Custine's book is strewn. It is clear that he, Turgenev, while unwilling to take the initiative in praising these judgments, is intrigued and excited by them, and would like to smell out Vyazemski's reactions.

M. Michel Cadot has mentioned, in his treatise,[19] the interesting possibility that Turgenev, Kozlovski, Chaadayev, and probably others as well, seized the occasion of Custine's visit to get before the European public a picture of the state of affairs in Russia which none of them was in a position to paint, but which they all wanted to see made known. If so, they must have been in part frightened by the results of their efforts; for the picture came out in colors obviously more lurid and dangerous than anything they had intended. All that the historian can say with assurance, at this juncture, is that the whole subject of Custine's Russian associations, and particularly his relations with Turgenev, is still surrounded with a number of intriguing mysteries, and will bear much further study.

VII. *CUSTINE IN RETROSPECT*

Shortly after delivery of my lectures on Custine at Oxford, I received a note from a Russian-born English acquaintance, Mr. Igor Vinogradoff, formerly an academic person and one for whose knowledge of the history of Russia in this period I had—and have—great respect. He had not heard the lectures but had read some of the notes from which I spoke. He wrote to warn against taking Custine too seriously and giving too much credit to the view of Russia he put forward. Custine, he wrote, was a "hysterical, discredited slanderer, crammed with Paris Polish mythology and 'Liberal,' i.e., Bonapartist or French Nationalist, *'rancunes.'*" Just because he had *deviné* the nightmare of Stalin, it did not follow that he was a truthful reporter of the reign of Nicholas I. His downright lies were less numerous than his wild generalizations or half- or quarter-truths, but his "frantic factual inaccuracy" alone made it impossible to treat him as a serious witness. He had simply profited by the generally anti-Russian prejudices then prevalent in England and France. This was the secret of his popular vogue at the time.

Mr. Vinogradoff went on to say some things about Nicholas I that certainly deserve attention in any consideration of Custine's work. A good deal, he pointed out, could be said in Nicholas' favor:

He believed in his own oath and in respecting other people's rights as well as his own; witness Poland before 1831 and Hungary in 1849. He hated serfdom at heart and would have liked to destroy it, as well as detesting the tyranny of the Baltic squires over their "emancipated" peasantry.

A military schoolmaster, of course, and a do-it-yourself monarch, of course. He must not be judged by the panic period of 1848-1855. He trusted very few men and tried to do the impossible with his own hands. But one should not forget that his Minister of Public Instruction was Uvarov . . . who did an immense amount to spread education through the Empire at all levels, and that he made Pushkin possible (even if he pinpricked him) and that he was delighted with "Revisor." A great literature blossomed in his reign. It was not for Polish Chauvinists . . . Bonapartist revanchards, Irish landlords, English sweatshop owners, and Indian nabobs to hold him up to contempt and ridicule. Yet it was they who inspired the enormous mass of Russian-hating literature, which the new middle classes swallowed with delight in England and France.

With most, if not all, of the above—and particularly the proposition that much injustice has been done in the treatment by liberal historians, not to mention the Communists, of the person of Nicholas I—I could agree. It is a view that is worthy of note in itself, as a qualified contemporary Russian commentary on the background of Custine's journey and book. But I adduce it here particularly as evidence that even the lapse of a century and a quarter have not sufficed to dim the vehemence of the negative and positive reactions evoked by *La Russie en 1839* or to cause it to lose its controversial actuality. It speaks in a sense for the importance of the issues raised by the book, if not of the book itself, that the challenge it presented—rightly or wrongly, fraudulently or with reason—continues to be felt as a challenge to people living one hundred and twenty-seven years after it was written. This being the case, no one who writes about the book today can avoid the obligation of forming and expressing his own view of its long-term significance.

Custine's book of course reflected, and reflected unfortunately, the various influences to which he was particularly subjected during and around the time of his journey. The trauma of the suppression of the Polish uprising of 1830-31 still affected in one way or another almost everyone with whom he was in close contact at that time. The atmosphere of the strongly Catholic milieu in which he circulated in Paris was deeply influenced by the partially distinguished and almost always eloquent figures of the new Polish emigration that now formed part of it; and these people, while capable of giving an informed picture of Russian society, had no interest in giving a balanced one. In his Russian contacts, on the other hand, Custine encountered the defensive edginess of previously liberal figures who had survived the Decembrist affair and lived to experience the severe strains which the Polish uprising placed upon their faith in their own country and their fading idealism. This state of the spirit, coming on top of the exaggerated Russian sense of prestige and congenital Russian self-consciousness in relations with western peoples, caused these Russian figures to over-react, made it difficult for them to discuss the problems of their own country in any relaxed and detached way, and stimulated that very combination of lofty pretension and secretive reticence which Custine found so intolerable. There was, finally, the unfortunate fact that Custine's questionable reputation had preceded him to Russia, that Russian noblemen were if anything even less tolerant than people in Paris towards the foibles with which his name was connected, and that he was never unaware of the glances and words that were being exchanged behind his back. All these factors tended to distort his response to the confrontation with Russia, causing him to underestimate what was good, to exaggerate, and to take pleasure in exaggerating, what was bad.

One must begin, therefore, by conceding the truth of a great deal of what was said by the unfavorable critics, particularly the Russian critics, about the weaknesses of Custine's book. It was, in the factual sense, dreadfully and almost shamefully inaccurate. He passed blithely on to his reader all the anecdotes and rumors and bits of hearsay that came his way, usually without serious effort at verification. He passed them on, I suspect, primarily to enliven the tale—as fragments of *Unterhaltungsliteratur*, designed to lighten the burden on the reader of the more serious philosophic reflections and psychological observations with which the account is studded. He let them stand as examples of the sort of gossip that might have met the ears of any western traveller as he moved through Russia. They were not really brought forward (and this is what the Victorian critics missed) to substantiate or illustrate the more serious reflections among which they were interspersed but rather to spare the reader the strain and tedium that would have been present if these reflections had been served up only in their pure form. Yet this was never explained. And in the absence of an explanation the listing of these hundreds of poorly-verified and often easily-disprovable items could not fail to damage the effectiveness of the work, provoking serious misunderstandings, and playing into the hands of ill-intentioned critics. It may well be argued that if Custine was going to bring forward what purported to be factual material, and if he was not going to label it as gossip and hearsay, then he owed it to his readers to see that it was really factual.

Nor were these the only weaknesses of the book, when taken as a commentary on the Russia of Nicholas I. The glimpse of Russian life that Custine had, during his brief journey, was of course wholly inadequate to the formation of any rounded view of the qualities of the Russian people or the nature of Russian society. Had he—once again— made this plain to his reader, and had he refrained from judgments on aspects of Russian life that he was not really qualified to judge, his case would have been stronger. The resulting errors and weaknesses in the book were partly ones of commission—of things he saw and interpreted wrongly; but they were more often ones of omission—of things, that is, that he did not see at all. He saw, in reality, only the social and official crust of Russian society. This,

to be sure, was one "Russia." There was another Russia—
one is tempted to say several other Russias—that he did
not see.

Take just his view of Russian literature. He saw something, to be sure, of the embittered older remnants of the
literary intelligentsia of the period of Alexander I (and
even these he greatly underrated); but he saw nothing of
the new literary intelligentsia that was coming along to
take its place. He had no idea of those resources of moral
earnestness and artistic vigor that would give to that bud-
ding coterie of great writers its eventual power. It was too
much to expect Custine to know that there was such a student as one Fedor Mikhailovich Dostoyevski in the School
of Military Engineering in Petersburg at the time when he
visited that city; or that there was developing, in the person
of a younger cousin of that same Alexander Turgenev who
gave him his letter of introduction, one of the really great
writers of the nineteenth century; or that on a country
estate, less than two hundred miles south of Moscow, there
was growing up a bright-eyed boy by the name of Lev,
full of fun and vitality, who was destined to become one
of the greatest, if not the greatest, novelists of all time.
Custine, of course, could not know these things as facts;
but he could, had his knowledge of Russia been deeper
and broader, have recognized them as possibilities—and
this he failed to do.

What he failed, then, to understand about the Russia of
his day was not the hypocrisy and pretentiousness of the
bureaucracy and the high society, particularly in its relationship to the West, and not the backwardness of a people
that had come late to the experiences of western civilization—these things he understood remarkably well; what
he failed to understand was the intensity of the awareness
of these weaknesses, the reaction against them, in some
instances the very shame of them, that existed in a great
many sadder, wiser, more modest, and more sensitive Russian minds. Not seeing this, he failed to understand that
the Russia he had before him did not represent the un-

opposed predominance of those tendencies and traits that so aroused his dislike, not the triumph of a heartless, arrogant autocracy over a dull-witted, spiritless people, but rather a momentous struggle, tragic in its implications, between two Russias: the Russia of power and cynicism, and the Russia of the spirit and faith.

It was this, not the recognition of much that was unworthy in Russian officialdom but the failure to recognize the intensity of the unhappiness over it in other echelons of Russian society, that caused so many Russians to cry out so indignantly against what Custine had written. Vyazemski, in his unpublished article, stated these feelings very well: "I am not saying," he wrote,

> that everything is for the best with us; . . . We know our own faults—know them much better than do our critics and detractors; we see all that we still lack as a daughter-nation of the great European family. We know that we have a great deal of work to do on ourselves and much more to achieve before we arrive at the point to which our efforts and our aspirations are directed. We do not propose to place ourselves, on our own initiative, at the head of civilization; we do not claim to be the tutors or the regents of other nations. But we too have our place in the sun, and it is not M. de Custine who is going to deprive us of it.

If, then, the question be posed in the form in which it was indeed posed by so many of the contemporary critics— could one have gained, that is, from Custine's book, an informed and fair picture of Russian society and of the strengths and weaknesses of the Russian people as of that time?—one would have to answer this question in the negative. Let us agree with the critics. Custine's work was not a very good book about the Russia of Nicholas I. It analyzed and depicted with pitiless sharpness certain of the inconsistencies and pretenses and false postures of the government and the high bureaucracy, but anyone looking to it, as well-educated Victorian Englishmen, in particular, were inclined to do, for a sort of compendium of sound factual information about a great and little-known country, or anyone seeking an informed analysis of the intellectual and spiritual qualities of the Russian people, was bound to be disappointed.

These demands were, perhaps, the only ones that many people of that time were able to place—or could have been expected to place—upon Custine's book. But they are not the only ones that must be raised by people of the 1960's and 1970's. For even if we admit that *La Russie en 1839* was not a very good book about Russia in 1839, we are confronted with the disturbing fact that it was an excellent book, probably in fact the best of books, about the Russia of Joseph Stalin, and not a bad book about the Russia of Brezhnev and Kosygin.

Does this fact require demonstration? Very little, surely. It is something that has been recognized by practically everyone who has had any knowledge of Stalin's Russia and who has then, in the light of that knowledge, read even the recent condensations of *La Russie en 1839*. Here, as though the book had been written yesterday (but in better and more striking language than most of us today would be able to command), appear all the familiar features of Stalinism: the absolute power of a single man; his power over thoughts as well as actions; the impermanence and un-substantiality of all subordinate distinctions of rank and dignity—the instantaneous transition from lofty station to disgrace and oblivion; the indecent association of syco-phancy upwards with brutality downwards; the utter dis-enfranchisement and helplessness of the popular masses; the nervous punishment of innocent people for the offenses they might be considered capable of committing rather than ones they had committed;* the neurotic relationship to the

---

* See *La Russie*, Letter 14, ɪɪ, 132: "Ambitious Russians will always take pleasure in killing a man. 'Let us strangle him by way of pre-caution,' they will say to one another. 'There will always be one less. A man, after all, is almost a rival, because, being human, he could

West; the frantic fear of foreign observation; the obsession with espionage; the secrecy; the systematic mystification; the general silence of intimidation; the preoccupation with appearances at the expense of reality; the systematic cultivation of falsehood as a weapon of policy; the tendency to rewrite the past. In the phenomenon of Stalinism all these features of the Russian scene, features which had impressed themselves only indistinctly on Custine's consciousness in 1839 like the fragments of an evil nightmare, would emerge a hundred years later in full and visible reality, no longer to be semi-concealed, no longer to bring blushes to the faces of their authors when attention was called to them, but now to be held brazenly aloft in the daylight as favored principles of political leadership, indispensable means of leading the Russian people, or any other people, down the broad vistas of utopian socialism. And along with all this there would go the semi-religious messianism, the pretension of universal validity for an official Russian faith, and the suppression of the liberties of neighboring peoples—the Poles in 1831, the Czechs in 1968—in the alleged interests of the internal security of the Russian state.

What are we to make of this strange anomaly: that the nightmare of 1839 should have become the reality of 1939, and the semi-reality of 1969? The answer to this question must be sought, surely, in the span of Russian history that linked the time of Custine with the time of Stalin. For three quarters of a century after the appearance of Custine's book, the development of government and politics in Russia was destined to be determined primarily by the competing efforts of three forces: (1) the diehard reactionaries who wanted no change at all—a faction to be found largely within the framework of governmental bureaucracy, but partly also within the ranks of the land-owning gentry and the senior military and police officials; (2) the liberals and democratic socialists, who wanted gradual reform and peaceful, organic progress—a faction to be found in small

---

always become one.'" (This is a free translation of the original, which does not lend itself to a literal one.)

part within the government, but mostly outside it, among the provincial gentry and the cream of the new intelligentsia; and (3) the revolutionary socialists and anarchists, people entirely outside the government, who wanted violent, sudden change—change by revolution, not by evolution. It must be noted that between the first and third of these categories there existed a certain bond of common purpose: neither wished to see the regime adjust to the demands of the modern age and evolve in the direction of greater liberality or a greater degree of popular representation and participation. It was the liberals alone who pursued this objective.

As among these three forces, Custine was able to see the first very clearly; and this, in the main, is what he described. He was also able dimly to sense, if not to see, the third. There are interesting passages in his work about the forces working towards revolution in Russia and the prospects for the success of their efforts. He was quite aware that there were, abroad though concealed in the Russia that lay before him, revolutionaries, conspiracies, secret societies, subterranean efforts to prepare the unseating of the regime. Such things, he thought, were in the nature of Russian society, and would long continue to exist. The great distances of the Empire were favorable, he astutely observed, both to revolt and to oppression.

He thought, too, that he could see something of the nature of these future revolutionaries. He pointed to a number of what he thought would be features of their position and personality: their classless status, their lack of social rootedness (many, he thought correctly, would be the sons of priests); their spotty and unfinished education; their lack of religious faith and ethical discipline; and the great moral and philosophical confusion of mind—the illusions of a total personal freedom, an absence of all ethical restraint in the pursuit of utopian objectives—that would inform and poison their activity.

He did not think the government would ever be overthrown by popular revolt—by an uprising of the people *en masse*—not, at any rate, so long as it remained consistently ruthless. One will recall (see Chapter V, pages 85-86) his melancholy conclusions in this respect:

> Nothing can really discredit authority in the eyes of a people where obedience has become a condition of life. . . . Clemency represents weakness in the approach to a people hardened by terror; nothing disarms such a people but fear; implacable severity forces it to its knees; mercy, on the contrary, causes it to raise its head; one would not know how to convince it; one can do no other than to subdue it; . . . [etc.].

But the popular uprising was not the only way a regime could be overthrown; and Custine also sensed the ultimate approach of revolution. He viewed it as the inevitable product of the abdication by the Russian nobility of its true function as the principal bulwark against tyranny. He could not predict its timing. He doubted that even the grandchildren of people then alive would witness it. But its eventual occurrence was something that seemed to him to be in the air.

He looked for no good to come of such a turn of events. It would be, he said, a revolution more terrible than the one (the French Revolution) of which Europe had just recently been the witness. And it would be all the more terrible, he thought, because it would be conducted in the name of religion. It would end with the confounding of Church with State—of heaven with earth. He was not entirely wrong in this judgment. He was wrong of course about the identity of the religion. It would be, in the final event, not the Christian Orthodoxy of the Eastern Rite, the one he so mistrusted, in the name of which the Revolution would be conducted, but a new secular orthodoxy called Marxism-Leninism, decidedly different in its philosophic inspiration but very little different from the pre-revolutionary Orthodox Russian Church in its relationship to the secular power, basing itself like its predecessor on a claim to be the executor of a species of scriptural revelation, creating its own population of saints, angels, martyrs, and devils, surrounding itself with a largely similar iconography, even down to the mummification of saints, and distinguished from its predecessor primarily by its concentration on the material aspects of existence here below, by its attempt to remove from the next world to this both the promise of heaven and the reality of hell.

Such was Custine's dim apprehension of the revolutionary tendencies in Russian society; and it was, as we see, not without its elements of accuracy. But we must note, at the same time, that if he had some idea of the first and third of the forces that were destined to shape the Russian future in the decades following publication of his book, he was wholly oblivious to the existence and the future power of the second—Russian liberalism. No wonder his book fell into oblivion or disrepute as the remainder of the nineteenth century ran its course. The power of liberal feeling in Russia, and the success it would have in moderating the autocracy, had no place in his view of the Russian future. Yet in those seventy-five years that were to elapse before the outbreak of the Russian Revolution, enormous changes would be brought about in Russian life under the pressure of liberal impulses—such changes as he himself would never have dreamed of. Serfdom would be abolished; and a promising beginning would be made—albeit only at the end of the period—on the correction of the evils of the organization of the agricultural process that serfdom had left in its train. A foundation would be laid for the development of proper organs of local self-government—something Russia had never before known. The judicial system would be reformed. Extensive civil rights would be established. A promising program of universal primary education would be undertaken, and in impressive degree completed. Eventually, even a parliament would be established—a parliament limited, to be sure, in its powers and in the scope of the suffrage from which it drew its composition, but not wholly powerless, not negligible as a modification of the autocracy and a factor in Russian life. And on top of all this, Russian culture—particularly literature, music, and the drama, but also science and intellectual life generally— would flourish as never before and never since, achieving for Russia, in these fields, a distinction not inferior to that of any of the great advanced western nations.

None of this, of course, had any place in Custine's view of Russia; and if some of his critics—Vyazemski, for example—could have lived down to 1914, they could have pointed, at that time, to this intervening span of Russian history as the refutation of the validity of Custine's view, insofar at least as it related to the prospects for Russia's future. They could have argued plausibly that those features of Russian life that impressed themselves so unfavorably on his consciousness were recessive ones, destined to be progressively weakened and overcome as Russia advanced into the modern age, and that those others which were really to shape Russian life most importantly over the coming decades were ones he had not seen at all. All of this would have been true; and if no change had occurred after 1914 to alter this liberal trend, we, at the turn of the seventh to the eighth decade of the twentieth century, could have dismissed Custine's book as a minor curiosity—an engaging false start—in the effort of western observers to understand the Russia of Nicholas I.

But 1917 and its consequences reversed this pattern. A curious and tragic conjunction of circumstances—an exhausting war; a weak and foolish Tsar; the impact of modern romanic nationalism on the non-Russian portions of the Empire—all converged to produce a virtual collapse of Tsardom in the most abnormal of circumstances. The liberals found themselves paralyzed by their commitment to a war effort that was embittering the peasantry, demoralizing the armed forces, playing at every point into the hands of the extremists on right and left. They found themselves in this way effectively without popular support at the crucial moment. The radical revolutionaries, as we all know, seized power with ease. Of their two adversaries, the reactionaries and the liberals, these revolutionaries had regarded the one with envy and contempt, the other with real hatred. They now destroyed them both, with an impartial callousness. In destroying the liberals, they also rejected everything the latter stood for. But in destroying the reactionaries, they did not reject entirely what these latter stood for; a great deal of it they appropriated for themselves, re-establishing, but in a more extreme form, even many of the outlooks and methods of rule that had characterized Russia long before Nicholas I. In more ways than one the removal of the center of power from Petersburg to Moscow restored the spirit and practices of the Grand Duchy of Muscovy: the defiant, xenophobic sense of religious orthodoxy, the breakdown of communication with the West, the messianic dreams of Moscow as the Third Rome, the terrible punishments, and the sultry, intrigue-laden air of the stuffy chambers of the Kremlin.

But it was precisely these archaic traits of the Russian political personality that stood out in Custine's view of Russia. It was the pale, fading afterglow of old Muscovy that he sensed in the Russia he saw before him. Many of these traits, to be sure, were already only latent in Russian society at the time he made his visit. Others were still to some extent active. But, active or latent, he had sensed and recorded them all, and it was to them that he had reacted. Now, in the wake of 1917, but above all with the triumph of Stalin in the late twenties, Bolshevik fanaticism, intolerance, and self-righteousness would evoke these archaic trends to life and would enthrone them once again, as fundamental principles of Russian government. And in doing so, it would unwittingly give to Custine's fevered reactions and apprehensions a reality and a validity they had never enjoyed when Custine himself was alive.

Now, it is a reasonable view (this writer, among others, adheres to it) that the Russian Revolution was fortuitous, insofar as it was the product of a number of factors in the sudden coming-together of which no logical pattern can be discerned. One can think of a number of individual circumstances any one of which might very easily, but for the hand of chance, have been quite different than it actually was—and different in such a way as to obviate the second Russian Revolution of 1917, if not the first. Had this happened, it is conceivable that the advance of Russia along liberal-democratic lines might have continued successfully, with the features of Custine's nightmare receding even further into the past—receding, in fact, to the point where they would have begun to appear as wholly and irrevocably archaic and the very thought of reviving them as principles of government in the modern age would have appeared absurd. This, I reiterate, *might* have happened. It was a possibility. And since it was only by action of the hand of chance that it did not happen, one could say, I suppose, that Custine's posthumous triumph was fortuitous, and therefore no great credit to his perspicacity.

There is something to be said for this view—but not everything. It was, after all, Russia, and no other country, about which Custine made these observations; and it was again Russia, and no other country, in which, a century later, they found their fulfillment. Whatever else may be said about Custine, and whichever of his many weaknesses may be held against him, his readers of the present age must concede that he detected, in the glimpse he had of Russia in the summer of 1839, traits in the mentality of Russian government and society, some active, some latent, the recognition and correction of which would be vital to the future success and security of Russian society—to its security, above all, not just against those external forces by whose fancied heretical will Russians of all ages have so easily seen themselves threatened, but rather its security against itself.

There are one or two afterthoughts that deserve attention before this discussion is concluded.

It was, as we have seen, a reproach that could justly be raised against Custine in his time that whereas a great deal of what he had seen in Russia, especially in the psychological and philosophical sense, really existed, a great deal also existed which he had not seen. There was, after all, the "other Russia"—the opposite pole to all the brutality, the callousness, the meanness of spirit that offended him.

I must emphasize that just because the negative pole has become superficially predominant in the Russia of 1970 does not mean that the other pole does not also still exist somewhere in the great mute depths of the Russian population. It is true the Bolsheviki have succeeded, over these fifty years, in destroying, or in driving out of Russia, a great deal of all that was liberal and humane and hopeful in the human material of which Russia, at the time of the Revolution, consisted. The forces of Russian liberalism, insofar as they have survived at all, have been largely drained off into other countries, to enrich the lives of other peoples as they impoverished, by their disappearance, that of Russia herself. It would be idle to suppose that the positive forces in Russian life have not been weakened by this reckless and savage prodigality on the part of the regime. If the negative pole of Russian life is stronger than it was in Custine's day, the positive pole, alas, must be presumed to be somewhat weaker.

But it is not wholly absent. And it is not beyond the possibility of re-creation. We must remember that the constructive forces which manifested themselves in Russia's late nineteenth- and early twentieth-century life had themselves emerged, at one time, out of tyranny and squalor and degradation. They too had their roots in what one would have thought was unhopeful soil. That they survived, and eventually manifested themselves, and grew, was the reflection of a certain ineradicable, defiant faith in the value of the human individual and meaningfulness of the human experience—a faith that has been reflected at a thousand points over these past two hundred years, and continues to be reflected regularly today, in what is the true medium of the Russian conscience—the literary word.

It is not the Russian people as a whole on whom it is incumbent to respond to the challenge Custine has raised, although it would be useful for all of them to reflect upon it. It is also not the ghosts of the rulers of 1839, to whose faults and virtues history has now given a better, and in general more favorable, appraisal than Custine was able to give. It is rather the present rulers of Russia—men who had their political origins in that Stalinist system which first gave reality to Custine's bad dreams and who have not been able to muster the courage or the enlightenment to reject this morbid heritage. They continue, by implication, to accept a moral responsibility for the conditions of Stalin's day as well as of their own. It is they, above all, who must face the question as to whether Custine's strictures were or were not—are or are not—without force.

REFERENCE NOTES

PREFACE

[1] This edition was entitled *Nikolayevskaya epokha. Vospominaniya frantsuskogo puteshestvennika—Markiza de Kyustina.* Moscow, Tovarishchestvo Skoropechatny A. A. Levinsona, 1910. It can be found in the Widener Library.

[2] *Nikolayevskaya Rossiya*, Moscow, 1910. This edition, a condensation in Russian translation, was put out by the Society of Former Political Prisoners and Exiles.

[3] In 1956 there appeared in Monaco, under the imprint of the Éditions du Rocher, a small volume entitled *Marquis de Custine, Souvenirs et Portraits. Textes choisis et presentés par Pierre de Lacretelle.* This volume included a valuable biographical introduction of 62 pages, from the pen of M. de Lacretelle. A year later, on the centennial of Custine's death, this was followed by the appearance, with the same publisher, of the first, and to date only, full-fledged (albeit brief) biography. This was written by the Marquis de Luppé, and was entitled simply *Astolphe de Custine.* The Marquis de Luppé, in addition to having collected a personal library of Custiniana, made extensive use of letters from and to Custine, as well as other documentary evidence, found in the personal archives of Custine's friends and acquaintances. His interest in Custine was evidently of long standing, for some thirty years earlier he had published a small volume of the latter's correspondence with the Marquis de la Grange.

I have not been able to establish the relationship between these two biographical works, published in such close succession by the same Monacan publisher. I must acknowledge, however, that aside from the question of the background and circumstances of the journey to Russia (in which connection my primary indebtedness to the work of M. Michel Cadot has been noted in the preface) it is almost exclusively to these two authors that I am indebted for what I am able to relate here concerning Custine's life and person.

CHAPTER I · *The Man*

[1] Custine's mother is mentioned in many sources, but particular note should be made of the volume by B.J.A. Bardoux: *Madame de*

Custine, d'après des documents inédits, Paris, 1888. For her relations with Chateaubriand, see particularly E. Chedieu de Robethon, *Chateaubriand et Madame de Custine,* Paris, Librairie Plon, 1893.

[2] Emmanuel de Lévis-Mirepoix, *Correspondance de la Marquise de Montcalm,* Paris, Éditions de Grand Siècle, 1949, p. 70.

[3] *Loc.cit.*

[4] *La Russie,* I, 162.

[5] The work in question was entitled *Mémoires et voyages; lettres écrites à diverses époques, pendant des courses en Suisse, en Calabre, en Angleterre et en Écosse.* It was published in Paris, by A. Vézard, in 1830, in four volumes.

[6] The account of the travels in Spain was published in Paris, in 1838, by the publisher Ladvocat, in four volumes, under the title *L'Espagne sous Ferdinand VII.*

CHAPTER II · *The Motives of the Journey*

[1] *L'Espagne sous Ferdinand VII,* vol. 2, p. 212 of the Brussels edition of 1838, end of Letter xxviii.

[2] These passages are taken from vol. III, pp. 424-426, of the collection of Balzac's correspondence (H. de Balzac, *Correspondance*) recently put out (this volume in 1964) by Éditions Garnier Frères, in Paris. In translation, the passages would read as follows:
The first:
. . . there are few modern books that could be compared with these letters.
I say this only between ourselves, but the book on Spain is a work that could not have been written by any of [our] professional *littérateurs.*
You are the traveller *par excellence.* What you write covers me with confusion, for it seems to me that I would be incapable of writing such pages.
And the second:
If you do the same thing for each country, you will have produced a unique collection of this sort, and one which, believe me, will have great value. This is a matter in which I know what I am talking about. I shall do everything in my power to get you committed to the description of Germany, the interior of Italy, Russia, and Prussia, in this manner. It will be a great book—and a great glory.

[3] Alexis de Tocqueville, *Democracy in America,* New York, Vintage Books, I, 452.

[4] This passage will be found in a letter from Custine to Varnhagen von Ense, dated February 22, 1841, as cited in *Marquis de Custine, Souvenirs et portraits,* ed. Pierre de Lacretelle, p. 219.

REFERENCE NOTES

[5] This passage will be found in Letter 5, *La Russie*, i, 120. In translation it would read as follows:

. . . these great spirits see only what they wish to see; their world is within them; they understand everything except that which one says to them.

[6] Berkeley and Los Angeles, University of California Press, 1955.

[7] For reference to this edition of Mickiewicz' work, see Jean Lorentowicz, *La Pologne en France. Essai d'une bibliographie raisonée*, Paris, 1935.

CHAPTER III · *Custine's "Road to Russia"*

[1] I am indebted to M. Cadot's work for the drawing of my attention to this letter, which will be found in the *Ostaf'evski Arkhiv*, vol. iv, p. 79, letter 832. (See footnote on p. 32.)

[2] I have taken the liberty, here, of making my own translation of these passages, taking them from the text published by M. Gershenzon, *P. Ya. Chaadayev. Zhizn i Myshlenie.*, S.-Peterburg: Tipografia M. M. Stasulevicha, 1908, p. 215.

[3] *La Russie*, i, 97-98.

[4] These passages will be found in the fifth of Custine's "letters," mostly in pages 140-145 of Volume i.

[5] *La Russie*, i, 146-147.

[6] *La Russie*, i, 191-193.

[7] I have taken this translation from the English text printed in the Appendix to Pushkin's *Bronze Horseman*, by the late Wacław Lednicki, Berkeley and Los Angeles, University of California Press, 1955, p. 139.

CHAPTER IV · *Custine in Russia*

[1] M. Cadot, *La Russie dans la vie intellectuelle française, 1839-1856*, Paris, Fayard, 1967, p. 276.

[2] These passages will be found in *La Russie*, iv, 30th letter.

[3] *La Russie* (3rd edition), iv, 59-60.

CHAPTER V · *The Book*

[1] *La Russie*, ii, 61.

[2] See *La Russie*, i, 138. The French original read as follows: "Imposer aux nations le gouvernement des majorités, c'est les soumettre à la médiocrité. Si tel n'est pas votre but, vous avez tort de vanter le gouvernement de la parole. La politique du grand nombre est presque toujours timide, avare, et mesquine."

[3] *La Russie*, i, xix.

[4] These passages recounting the conversation with the Emperor will be found in *La Russie*, ii, 46 and 47.

[5] Anna Maria Rubino, *Alla Ricerca di Astolphe de Custine*, Edizioni di Storia e Letteratura, Rome, 1968, p. 153.

[6] *La Russie*, III, 338.

[7] *Ibid.*, I, 185.

[8] *Ibid.*, II, 114.

[9] *Ibid.*, I, 253-254.

[10] *Ibid.*, I, 273.

[11] *Ibid.*, II, 109-110.

[12] *Ibid.*, I, 6.

[13] *Ibid.*, I, 5.

[14] *Ibid.*, II, 133.

[15] See *La Russie*, II, 328: "Ce sont des ours façonnés qui me font regretter des ours bruts; ils ne sont pas encore des hommes cultivés, qu'ils sont déjà des sauvages gâtés." Again, I, 303: "Alors je me dis: voilà des hommes perdus pour l'état sauvage et manqués pour la civilisation. . . ."

[16] I have taken the liberty of combining here two of Custine's passages. For the reference to the theatre, see *La Russie*, II, 360; for the remainder, I, 288.

[17] Again, I have combined passages. For the first sentence, see *La Russie*, I, 303; for the second, II, 209; for the third, I, 191.

[18] *La Russie*, II, 121.

[19] These sentences are all taken from the statements of the Russian prince whom Custine met on the ship, as recounted in Volume I of *La Russie*, but I have taken the liberty of changing their order. For the first, see p. 143; for the second, p. 184; for the third, p. 183.

[20] *La Russie*, II, 119.

[21] *Ibid.*, II, 134-135.

[22] *Ibid.*, II, 134.

[23] *Ibid.*, II, 157.

[24] *Ibid.*, I, 143.

[25] *Ibid.*, II, 321. I have used in part, here, the language of the Longman edition.

[26] *Ibid.*, II, 244. In this case, I have taken the translation entirely from that which appeared in an article entitled "Through the Russian Looking-Glass," from the pen of my good friend Lewis Galantiere, which appeared in the quarterly *Foreign Affairs* of October 1949, pp. 122 and 123.

[27] *Ibid.*, II, 321. The translation here is again that of the Longman edition.

[28] *Ibid.*, I, 321. Again, the Longman translation.

[29] *Ibid.*, I, 254.

[30] *Ibid.*, II, 119.

[31] *Ibid.*, I, 288.

[32] *Ibid.*, II, 382.

[33] *Ibid.*, II, 383.

[34] *Ibid.*, III, 337.
[35] *Ibid.*, III, 58.
[36] *Ibid.*, II, 364.
[37] *Ibid.*, II, 384.
[38] *Ibid.*, II, 313.
[39] *Ibid.*, I, 267-268.
[40] For the full account of Kozlovski's reflections on Russian history, see the fifth of Custine's "letters," I, 140-147.
[41] *La Russie*, IV, 355.
[42] *Ibid.*, IV, 354. For this great passage, as well as for the immediately preceding one, I have availed myself, with one or two minor modifications, of the Longman translation, to be found on page 521 of the 1854 edition.
[43] *Ibid.*, II, 314.
[44] *Ibid.*, II, 314.
[45] *Ibid.*, II, 314-317. For the second of these paragraphs I have used again, with minor modifications, the Longman translation.
[46] *Ibid.*, I, 148-149. I have taken the liberty, here, of reversing the order of the two passages. The first, as shown here, will be found on p. 149, the other on p. 148.
[47] *Ibid.*, I, 152.
[48] Page 499, of the Longman, 1854, edition. I have retained in this and in the following passage, the original punctuation of the Longman edition.
[49] *Ibid.*, p. 493.
[50] *La Russie*, IV, 80-81.
[51] *Ibid.*, IV, 193-195.

CHAPTER VI · *The Reaction to* Russia in 1839

[1] Cited by Cadot, *La Russie dans la vie intellectuelle française*, p. 251.
[2] Article by Serge Fleury, "Custine et Madame Récamier," *Revue des Études Historiques*, January-March 1929, 95th year, p. 187.
[3] J. Yakovlev (pseudonym), *La Russie en 1839 rêvée par M. de Custine*, Paris, Chez les principaux libraires, 1844, p. 46.
[4] Mikhail Lemke, *Nikolayevskie Zhandarmy*, St. Petersburg, 1909, p. 147.
[5] *Pis'ma Aleksandra Turgeneva Bulgakovym*, Moscow, Gosudarstvennoe Sotsial'no-Ekonomicheskoe Izdatel'stvo, 1939 (see note on p. 32 above), p. 268; letter of A. Turgenev to Bulgakov, Dec. 26/ Jan. 7, 1843/44.
[6] Chaudes-Aigues' review will be found in the *Revue de Paris*, Vol. 24, 4th series, 1843.
[7] *Literaturnoe Nasledstvo*, Nos. 31-32, Moscow, Zhurnal'no-gazetnoe Ob'edinenie, 1937. Article entitled "Balzak v Rossii," p. 155.

[8] Cadot, *La Russie dans la vie intellectuelle française,* pp. 265-278.

[9] *Pis'ma Aleksandra Turgeneva Bulgakovym,* pp. 263-264, letter of A. Turgenev to A. Bulgakov, Dec. 11/23, 1843.

[10] Cited by Cadot from the *Ostaf'evski Arkhiv,* in *La Russie dans la vie intellectuelle française,* pp. 236-237.

[11] *Edinburgh Review,* April 1844.

[12] Cadot, *La Russie dans la vie intellectuelle française,* p. 228.

[13] *Quarterly Review,* vol. 73, 1844, pp. 324-27.

[14] *La Russie,* II, 94.

[15] *La Russie,* IV (3rd edition), 371.

[16] *Pis'ma Aleksandra Turgeneva Bulgakovym,* p. 261, letter of A. Turgenev to A. Bulgakov, July 30/Aug. 11, 1843.

[17] Cited in Cadot, *La Russie dans la vie,* from *Ostaf'evski Arkhiv,* p. 256; letter 944.

[18] *Pis'ma Aleksandra Turgeneva Bulgakovym,* p. 265, letter of A. Turgenev to A. Bulgakov, Dec. 12/24, 1843.

[19] Cadot, *La Russie dans la vie,* p. 208.

INDEX

In the case of Russian names, given and patronymic, the exact Russian transliteration has been used wherever the patronym is included and in all other instances except where, as for example in the case of Alexander Pushkin, there is a common and widely-employed anglicization of the first name.

INDEX

Nizhni Novgorod, Custine's visit
to, 38, 63, 66, 67

Odoyevski, (Prince) Vladimir
Fedorovich, 35, 37, 54, 60,
61, 66n
Oldenburg, Duchess of, 58
*Ostaf'evski Arkhiv Knyazei
Vyazemskikh* (Archive of the
Vyazemski family from the
estate of Ostaf'evo), 32n
Ostrowski, Christian, translator of
Mickiewicz, 28

Paskevich, (Marshal, Prince)
Ivan Fedorovich, Viceroy in
Poland, 45, 45n, 47, 68
Peter the Great, Russian Tsar,
115n
Peterhof, Custine's visit to,
58, 78
Petersburg, Custine's visits to,
and views about, 55-61, 67, 87;
views of Pushkin and
Mickiewicz with regard to, 53
*Pis'ma Aleksandra Turgeneva
Bulgakovym* (Letters of
Alexander Turgenev to the
Bulgakovs), 32n
Poland, Polish influences on
Custine, 23-29, 36, 37, 43, 44,
54, 64, 68, 116, 118-120;
uprising of 1830-31, 33, 36,
48, 51, 52, 74, 75, 120, 125
Poltoratski, (General) K. M.,
Governor at Yaroslavl, 66, 67
Pushkin, Alexander, 11, 27n,
34-37, 45, 47, 48, 51, 52-54,
57, 119

Quarterly Review, 110
Quotidienne, 105

Rachel, Elisa Felix, French
actress, 24
Radolinska, Countess, 26, 27n
Rahel, wife of Varnhagen von
Ense, 5, 35
Récamier, (Madame) Pauline,
9, 21, 35, 36, 75n

Revolution, Russian, of 1917,
127-131
Revue de Paris, 104, 105
Richelieu, Madame de, *see*
Montcalm-Gozon
Roman Catholic Church, its
influence on Custine, 7, 16,
40, 41, 44, 47, 54, 109, 120

St. Barbe, Edward, *see*
Sainte-Barbe
St. Gratien, home of Astolphe de
Custine, 13
Saint-Marc Girardin, *see* Girardin
Sainte-Barbe, Édouard de, 8,
9, 13
Sand, George, 9, 26
Schlüsselburg, Custine's visit to
fortress of, 59, 60
Scotland, Custine's travels in, 12
Scott, (Sir) Walter, 11
Shcherbatov, (Prince), 45n
Shcherbatova, (Princess) E. D.,
62
Simbirsk, peasant disorders in,
64, 65
Smith, (General) Walter Bedell,
viiin
Société Typographique Belge,
Belgian publishing house, 95,
98, 103n
Southern Quarterly Review, 111
Spain, Custine's travels in, 12,
15, 16, 18
Staël, Madame de, 4
Stalin, Iosif Vissarionovich, 124,
130
Stendhal (Marie Henri Beyle), 9
Struve, (Professor) Gleb, viiin,
47, 47n, 48
Sverbeyev, Dmitri Nikolayevich,
41, 62
Sverbeyeva, Katerina
Aleksandrovna, 35, 41
Switzerland, Custine's travels in,
12, 71

Talleyrand-Périgord, Charles
Maurice de, 5